Grace, Race, and the Church:
Sharing Our Stories Family Style

Edited by Tom Sugimura

DEDICATION

To the members of New Life Church
for sharing your stories and your lives with Christ-like grace and truth

And to Angela and Nathan Warner
for making a difference in your chosen community one student at a time

TABLE OF CONTENTS

FOREWORD

One of the most painful, yet impactful conversations in my life was when a seminary mentor and fellow pastor shared with me about the Sunday morning a young, black family visited his all-white church in Atlanta, Georgia. He shared how he gently, but firmly, told them that they would "feel more comfortable" attending another church than his. I was appalled, hurt, and profoundly disappointed because he was a dear friend and biblical scholar whom I greatly respected. Yet I hurt even more because of my deep love for the church—a love that was shaped by my childhood experiences with God's people.

Located in the northwest corner of Columbus, Ohio, my childhood church was a diverse congregation of people from every race and socioeconomic background. There were yellow, black, brown, and white brothers and sisters. There were long-haired hippies, well-dressed military personnel, and stellar college athletes. There were those who were very well off and others who were struggling just to make it. I still remember looking across the aisles to see a number of precious young adults with severe mental and physical handicaps. Even as a child, I knew that anyone and everyone was welcome in our church. I knew intuitively that our church family was a reflection of the heart of God and His love for all of humanity. I also knew that my seminary mentor had missed it. He had missed the very heart of God. These words are painful for me to say about a dear friend, but I say them based on the words of Scripture.

The moment we open the Bible, God reveals His heart to unite all things unto Him. Paul makes this undeniably clear in his letter to the church in Ephesus, telling us that the "mystery of God's will" is to "unite all things in heaven and on earth" by breaking down the "dividing wall of hostility" between Jews and Gentile and reconciling all believers to Christ "through the cross." Paul continues, telling us that it is God's plan to make the mystery of His will known "through the church." The church, then, is to be a reflection of the heart of God when His beautifully diverse children are united together as one in Christ. As Paul also wrote to the church in Galatia, "There is neither Jew nor Gentile, neither free nor slave, nor is there male and female, for you are all one in Christ Jesus." This Good News is clear. Through the blood of Christ, we have been reconciled to God AND to one another, and the church is to reflect this Good News for all the world to see. This Good News entails not only our reconciliation with God, but also with one another. Ironically, my seminary mentor and friend missed this biblical truth in the very shadow of Martin Luther King's former church in Atlanta, even though Dr. King had given his life for people to come together as brothers and sisters. Tragically, my fellow pastor missed it in the very shadow of the cross where Jesus died to save us from our sins AND to seal us together as one in Him. He missed it. He missed it. But while my seminary mentor missed it, he is surely not alone.

Throughout the ages, the church has often missed God's heart for us. We miss it when we sing of the blood of Christ shed to make us one while remaining racially segregated. We miss it when we sing of the church's "one foundation" while remaining ethnically divided and even reinforcing our separateness by referring to the "black church," the "white church," the "Hispanic church," or the "Asian church." We miss it when we allow all races into the church, but don't take the time to build deep relationships with people outside our own race. And horrifically, we miss it when we twist and distort the Scriptures to somehow justify our separateness in the body of Christ. Oh God, forgive us! And while recent studies show that the number of multiracial churches has increased from 7% in 1998 to 13% in 2010, I cannot help but think that the apostle Paul would be appalled at such a low percentage, especially in light of his clear teaching on the blood of Jesus, shed to break down the dividing wall of hostility. In so many ways, we are guilty of missing God's heart for His church, and I am regretfully a part of that guilty verdict.

For years, I prided myself on "loving everyone." When I stopped to examine my own circle of friends, however, I recognized that I needed to repent because they were all so much like me. I needed to repent because my homogeneous friend group revealed my own personal prejudices. I did not really love "everyone," I only spoke of it. So God had to move me from my white, suburban neighborhood in Tucson, Arizona with its backyard mountain view to inner-city Watts in South-Central Los Angeles with a front yard view of the Imperial Courts housing "projects" in order to cleanse me of my prideful prejudice. While that move has helped me to grow in my love for "everyone," I know that God still has much work to do in me to make my heart a better reflection of His. As Paul urges, I know that I must continue in my eagerness to maintain unity in the church and must continually ask God to purify my heart and my love for His people. I thank God for His mercy and patience in my life. I thank God for brothers like Tom Sugimura and for his encouragement to pursue the heart of God.

I have known Tom for several years as a friend and fellow pastor. Tom has a calm, confident, approachable demeanor with a truly humble spirit. These are the very attributes needed to build relationships across racial lines and to be a part of fulfilling God's plan for His people. I thank God for Tom's intentional efforts and his soft heart. I pray that God will use this work to make His heart known through the church and to unite His children as one in Him. I also pray that God will use this work to bring about accountability and healing for times when we have missed it. This is not a footnote in the Scriptures. Oneness in Christ is at the heart of the Gospel and I do not want to miss it. I do not want to miss it because Jesus died for it. I do not want to miss the heart of God and, if you are reading this book, I trust that you do not want to miss it either. Thank you, Tom, for being a brother and for helping us "get it"—to get the heart of God and His will which unites us together in His Son and through His church. To Him be the glory!

Todd Grant
Pastor of Watts Powerhouse Church
Director of Envision LA

CHURCH, LET'S TALK ABOUT RACE

"**M**y pastor hasn't addressed the race issue to my liking, so I don't intend to go back."

"We can't stay in a church that supports #BLM or Marxist ideology."

"11 o'clock on Sunday morning is one of the most segregated hours, if not the most segregated hour in Christian America."[1]

"Being in ethnic-specific context is not only permissible, it's actually quite necessary for a lot of Christians."[2]

It seems almost everyone has a different view on race. Yet race issues can be just as sensitive in today's church as they have been throughout history. These highly charged disputes often evoke defensiveness, apathy, rage, or fear. As a result, many of us ignore the matter entirely, either by treating it as taboo or by congregating only with people like ourselves. We avoid the subject until our fear of even talking about race demeans the "power of God for salvation to everyone who believes, to the Jew first and also to the Greek" (Romans 1:16).[3]

Some of us, however, talk about race so often it consumes our thoughts and overshadows our identity as followers of Christ. Such conversations also rarely happen face-to-face within the family of Christ's church. We

---

[1] Martin Luther King, Jr., "Meet the Press" interview, April 17, 1960, accessed at https://www.youtube.com/watch?v=1q881g1L_d8.

[2] Thabiti Anyabwile, "Why Ethnic-Specific Churches are Still Important: An Interview with Pastor Thabiti Anyabwile and Dr. Alexander Jun," *SOLA Network*, January 25, 2021, accessed at https://sola.network/article/why-ethnic-specific-churches-still-important-interview.

[3] All Scripture passages have been cited in the English Standard Version unless otherwise noted.

resort to flinging accusations and assumptions from afar. We attribute sound bites and social media blasts as the entirety of people's views. We listen mainly to our chosen tribe instead of our fellow believers who entrust us with their stories. We separate from those who address race issues either too much or too little for our liking. Yet such division should never happen among those united in Christ's body (1 Corinthians 12:25).

Instead, the story of good news in Jesus Christ must transcend each one of our personal stories. As Paul declared of the church, "Here there is not Greek and Jew, circumcised and uncircumcised, barbarian, Scythian, slave, free; but Christ is all, and in all" (Colossians 3:11).[4] Paul is not claiming the absence of these differences, but rather the subordination of these differences to our primary identity in Christ. Fellow believers must learn to share our varied stories from the common ground of gospel unity and testify to God's greater story of sinner, sufferer, and sovereign Savior.[5] So let's show grace to one another as we ask each other's stories, address our conflicts in the context of community, and affirm before the world God's greater glory.

Even if you are not a follower of Christ today, we gratefully invite you

---

[4] Scripture teaches that all of us belong to a single human race descended from Adam and that our Creator has distributed different people groups (or *ethnē*) throughout the earth (Acts 17:26). Racial prejudice, however, as depicted in God's Word, creates a socially constructed divide outside the Creator's sovereign plan. When sinners discriminate against each other on the basis of cultural background (e.g., Esther 3; James 2:1-9), racism is just one more egregious example of prideful partiality.

[5] Human beings have always sought the key to explain the individual stories within a movement. Some pit the oppressor against the oppressed to explain inequalities in race, class, or gender. Others tout humanistic evolutionary models as the basis for secular morality. Yet the biblical view presents every one of us as image-bearers of God navigating a world corrupted by original sin. We all suffer due to the fallenness of this age, our own personal wrongdoing, or the afflictions of self-interested others. All of us, therefore, need a sovereign Savior who momentarily allows this suffering for his good purposes, but will ultimately rescue his people from the consequences of sin. He will ultimately usher us into eternal glory where sin and suffering are no more. Christians believe that this gospel metanarrative explains every human story more fully than any other competing story (whether or not we as participants realize or accept it).

to enter this conversation. In fact, we share our stories to persuade you of a better way, to depict the beauty of the biblical worldview, and to rejoice in this glorious diversity within Christ's church. We have written not as experts, but as learners ourselves and with the assumption that many are new to the discussion. As you engage with us, you may not fully agree with the biblical truths expressed, but we urge you to consider them with an open mind.[6] If you are willing, we also encourage you to ask God in a simple prayer to change your thinking on these matters in conformity to what is true. Then may God's grace within all our stories compel us to embrace Christ Jesus and his church.

Ask Each Other's Stories

Jesus loved to help people tell their stories even though, as their Creator, he already knew them intimately. Our Lord and Savior knows his children each by name (Isaiah 43:1-2; John 10:3) and discerns our inmost thoughts (Psalm 139:1-4; Acts 15:8-9). Yet still, he delights to hear us share about ourselves. He listened to rabbi Nicodemus (John 3) just as he listened to the woman from Samaria (John 4). Likewise, he urges his church to listen well to others. In the words of Dr. King, "People fail to get along because they fear each other; they fear each other because they don't know each other; they don't know each other because they have not communicated with each other."[7] Stories teach us, as C.S. Lewis wrote, "to steal past watchful dragons."[8] They have the power to break down walls

---

[6] "Stories matter. Many stories matter. Stories have been used to dispossess and malign, but stories can also be used to empower and to humanize. Stories can break the dignity of a people, but stories can also repair that broken dignity." Yet only our Creator's story can fully explain the realities of this world, so we must not let any one human story define our understanding (Chimamanda Ngozi Adichie, "The Danger of a Single Story," *TED Global Conference* [2009], accessed at https://www.ted.com/talks/chimamanda_ngozi_adichie_the_danger_of_a_singl e_story).

[7] Martin Luther King, Jr., "Advice for Living," *Ebony Magazine* (May 1958), 112.

[8] Lewis made this reference in "Sometimes Fairy Stories May Say Best What's

and the power to unite. So let's start sharing our stories about race and culture:

- How has your family upbringing influenced you to think and talk about ethnicity?
- When did you first become a follower of Christ? How has gospel grace affected your interaction with God and with each other?
- What blessings or struggles have you encountered because of diversity in your church or in the community where you live?

Let's affirm when we have heard each other clearly and resist the temptation to judge with haste (Matthew 7:1-5). Let's also clarify our definitions and begin the conversation in the spaces we agree.[9] Let's read widely and generously to understand each other's differing views, for we will honor our fellow believers by listening well as they honor us by sharing (Romans 12:10).

In the following pages, members of the church I pastor share their testimonies of how Christ and culture have come together in their life experiences. Each of these storytellers claims a personal relationship with Jesus Christ as Lord (10:9, 13) and affirms that the biblical story of God's Word continues to shape our individual stories. Each of us are destined for glory in God's eternal kingdom, but we have all entered the conversation at different stages in our journey. As we stoke your thoughts, we hope that you will share your story as well in the context of a local church.

New Life Church began when a predominately Asian American leadership team helped revitalize a predominantly white historic congregation.[10] Our initial fellowship gatherings and especially potlucks

---

To Be Said," *New York Times* (November 18, 1956) to explain how stories often carry greater power than theological essays.

[9] See Appendix 1 for a list of working definitions to start the conversation.

[10] Although many of us were born overseas or into specifically ethnic families, our church is situated in diverse Southern California where the intermixing of cultures is more likely to happen. Multiethnicity need not be the primary goal of every church, although we should pray to reflect the makeup of our community.

were somewhat awkward, but we are learning to normalize diversity. We accept that some will pass us by when they see our pictures on the website, the foreignness of my last name, or the uncomfortable diversity of our Sunday worship. Yet still, we celebrate cultural dinners where each guest brings a representation of their culinary heritage. We welcome Greenhouse church planting families who teach us to care about and to pray for far-off reaches of the world like India, China, Estonia, Ethiopia, and Jackson, Mississippi. We partner with a denomination that ministers to unreached people groups beyond the borders of this nation. Yet we are by no means a perfect church. We have seen friends part ways over racial issues and some of us clique mainly with those who look like us. Others put politics before the way of Christ or listen only to pundits who reinforce our biases. Some have told blacks not to talk about race in the church when the whole nation was talking about #BlackLivesMatter. Others have claimed victimhood for race issues when those conflicts actually occurred for more complex reasons. Certain parents have struggled to watch their children marry a spouse of a different ethnicity. More commonly, however, we just don't see the problems. We claim that race is no longer an issue in our society or in the church. We don't recognize the subtle ways our decisions and our lifestyles are steeped in privilege. We don't address injustice because most of us rarely face it ourselves. We overlook the daily struggle of racialized communities and make choices without considering how they impact others. We are mostly unaware when discrimination does occur (even in the church) and sometimes we feel more multicolored than multicultural. Yet we accept that the church will never reach perfection until Christ returns again. So we ask forgiveness for our blind spots and make the Spirit-empowered effort to grow more and more like Jesus every day (2 Corinthians 3:18).

Each one of our storied lives are like brush strokes in the Grand Designer's artistic masterpiece (Ephesians 2:10). No one stroke defines another as they blend together in an integrated whole. Thus, we rejoice in our Creator, who wields such different shades and textures in his artistic palette. We realize that certain strokes will resonate more closely to your own, yet no experience is meant to be the final word. Our desire instead has been to start up conversations and not to shut them down. Most importantly, we thank our Lord and Savior Jesus Christ for the privilege of sharing our lives together as we have shared them in these pages.

Address Your Conflicts in Community

As followers of Jesus share our stories, conflict is certain to arise. Therefore, we must address them in a community shaped by grace and peace (Galatians 1:3). Our God, who has made us each uniquely in his image, receives all glory when diverse peoples, nations, tribes, and tongues declare his praise as one (Revelation 7:9-10). So let's remind each other often, especially in times of conflict, that we are brothers and sisters committed to community. Let's take each other by the hand instead of by the throat, for Jesus calls us to this "ministry of reconciliation" before any genuine change takes place (2 Corinthians 5:18).

This year, our church has gathered at the One Table Family Fellowship in Watts with fifteen other Bible-believing, Christ-exalting churches. We have fellowshipped over food, worship, and conversations about race. We've met individuals from different ethnic, cultural, and socioeconomic backgrounds and listened to their stories as we shared ours. We have also taken tiny faith-filled steps toward one another to show how the gospel which unites is stronger than the differences which divide. In this way, our hearts have been gradually transformed not just through additional information, but by investing deeper in community. We are learning to walk with empathy in each other's shoes and to share each other's burdens. We are asking questions even when we disagree and have allowed Christ's strength in us to bear the weight of our differing views.[11]

---

[11] The power of story has often been wielded by a fallen world to turn people further from the gospel, the community of Christ, and our Creator's glory. The church refutes such worldly "philosophy and empty deceit" (Colossians 2:8), but we must also tell a better story that can resonate with every person's smaller story. Only by walking in step with gospel grace can we avoid the works-based

May Christ's church continue to speak and act toward one another with the grace that God has shown to us (1 Corinthians 1:3-5). Then even as we disagree, let's do so with the goal of gently restoring unity (Galatians 6:1). Let's address our conflicts in community until our stories speak forth life instead of death (Proverbs 18:21). "Behold, how good and pleasant it is when brothers dwell in unity!" (Psalm 133:1).

Affirm God's Greater Story

As Christians tell and retell our stories within the context of God's greater story, we affirm the Bible's overarching narrative of Creation, Fall, Redemption, and New Creation.[12] Racial strife and social injustice are not how God created this world to be (Genesis 1-2). Yet the story of human suffering explains each conflict from the fall of man (ch. 3) until the present day (i.e., Cain and Abel, the tower of Babel, the Hebrew enslavement in Egypt, the Jerusalem Council, the Galatian controversy). God's all-sufficient grace in Christ then becomes our starting point for addressing race in the context of community (Ephesians 2:11-22). Thus, we are united not only by the fallenness of our past, but also by Christ's forgiveness of our sin and his promise of eternal life.

As we have listened to each other's stories, we learned that many of us had first been introduced to an imperfect, yet loving, Christian church through an ethnic-specific ministry or a unique cultural experience. We attended a Filipino church so we could speak with others in both English and Tagalog. We joined a black church so our children would have more role models who shared the color of our skin. Yet in those local churches,

---

approaches which seek to change behavior without addressing the heart. Only gospel grace emphasizes both the individual's responsibility to receive salvation in Jesus Christ (vv. 1-3) and the corporate responsibility of the redeemed church to live out their commitment of faith and justice (vv. 11-22).

[12] "New Creation" identifies the final state as more than simply a restoration of the old creation or a perfected consummation without relation to the old. The final state will be a new and better version of God's original design (see Makoto Fujimura, *Art and Faith: A Theology of Making* [New Haven, CT: Yale University Press, 2021]).

we learned the gospel which then transformed our understanding of racial identity. Culture brought us before the throne of Christ, then Christ renewed the ways we interact with culture.

So, as we take this journey, let's affirm God's greater story and care for one another by graciously asking, "How does your story fit into our Creator's? How does your life bring him greater glory?" (Colossians 3:17). We can minister to one another as we build their trust, listen actively, and ask good questions. Some friends may want us to lament (Romans 12:15b) and others just to stand beside them (Ecclesiastes 4:12). A few will seek our counsel from the Scriptures (Romans 15:14), while others need Christ's comfort (2 Corinthians 1:3-5). Whatever role we serve as we affirm God's greater story, let's tell it through his voice (John 10:27). Then let's be like Jesus as we explore grace, race, and the church together.

Questions for Reflection:

1. What makes it so difficult, even in the church, for people to talk about racial issues? How can we begin to break down barriers?

2. How does racial reconciliation among fellow Christians shine forth the light of Jesus and provide opportunities for gospel evangelism (Matthew 5:14-16; 2 Corinthians 4:5-7)? Why must reconciliation first take place between God and man before it can be accomplished between fellow image-bearers (2 Corinthians 5:17-21)?

HOPE BEHIND BARBED WIRE
Tom Sugimura

I could tell you my story.

Life in the Camp

I could tell you how the bombs dropped from Japanese planes and destroyed Pearl Harbor in the early hours of December 6, 1941. I could tell you how America, the sleeping giant, roused for war and imprisoned my father's parents in a concentration camp called Manzanar. I could tell you how we were tagged as family number 5112 and sent away with only the luggage we could carry in our hands. I could tell you how nearly 120,000 Japanese Americans had every possession and every dignity taken from the lives which they had worked so hard to build. I could tell you how it felt to be ostracized by an entire country along with all its churches, neighborhoods, and lawfully appointed authorities.

I could tell you also how it took forty years and a generation of silence for the U.S. government to declare this particular season of infamy as the product of "race prejudice, war hysteria, and a failure of political leadership."[1] I could tell you my story and it would resonate with you who have been unjustly treated and discriminated against.

Life on the Farm

Yet I could then tell you how my father's parents relocated to the farming community of Seabrook, New Jersey.[2] Seabrook was the only place to offer them an early exit from the camps, though living conditions were not much more improved. My grandparents worked alternating 13-hour

---

[1] Commission on Wartime Relocation and Internment of Citizens, *Personal Justice Denied* (Washington, D.C.: U.S. Government Printing Office, 1982), 18. I tell these stories more fully in *The Church Behind Barbed Wire: Stories of Faith During the Japanese American Internment of World War II* (Amazon, 2022).

[2] "Seabrook Farms," *Densho Encyclopedia,* accessed at https://encyclopedia.densho.org/Seabrook_Farms.

shifts (seven days a week) in Mr. Seabrook's Frozen Food Factory, so my father and his siblings often watched themselves. Still, however, there was food on the table every day, climbing roses outside their front window, and enough money scraped together to give the kids an education. There was also a tiny Christian church in Seabrook where my father heard the good news of Jesus and became the first in his family to follow Christ.

Lost and Found

My father's faith matured in college where he met a young woman who soon became his wife. My parents would then raise three children in a Christian home and teach us to trust in Jesus from an early age. My family's story is one of hope first lost, then found as God's greater story continues to unfold in every generation. Like Joseph, we can say of those who hurt us: "You meant evil against me, but God meant it for good, to bring it about that many people should be kept alive, as they are today" (Genesis 15:20).

The following stories told by members in my church reflect God's grace as we have thought and spoken about race together as a family. I thank the Lord for the courage of those who have shared their stories within these pages and grieve for those whose stories still cannot be spoken. We do not all agree on every element of our stories, but we have sought to "speak the truth in love" as we humbly learn from one another (Ephesians 4:15). So may these edifying words "give grace to those who hear" (v. 29).

Questions for Reflection:

1. Why were most Christian churches silent or even complicit in the mass incarceration of 120,000 Japanese Americans?

2. Was it right for the U.S. government to issue a formal apology and reparations to surviving internees? Does God require later generations to repent or make reparations for past sins against our fellow man?

THE KINDNESS OF A WHITE MAN
Tom Sugimura

My mother's parents, Kay Jen and Yun Yee Tom, were born in the Toishan region near the city of Canton (modern-day Guangzhou).[1] Like many young men his age, Kay Jen fled the poverty of southern China in the 1920's to seek his fortune in the land of "gold mountain." It was rumored that he stowed away on a ship which docked at Angel Island in the San Francisco Bay. He was detained and interrogated for weeks before receiving permission to disembark and begin his new life in America. Over the years, he trekked from place to place, finding kitchen jobs in hotels and restaurants from California to Montana. Eventually, he became a U.S. citizen and served as a cook on a survey team to Alaska during the WWII years. After that, he leased a cafeteria from the Continental Can Company in East Oakland and began to save his earnings.

By the late 1940's, men were legally permitted to bring over wives from China.[2] So Kay Jen sent his picture to the village matchmaker in Toishan to find him a wife and Yun Yee took a risk that living with a stranger would be better than laboring in the rice fields. They met in Hong Kong and were married in May 1949 just months before China became a communist country. She was 26 and he was 39 (ten years older than the picture he had sent to woo her).

God's Providence

In 1954, my grandparents bought their first home in East Oakland and, three years later, sent my mom and her brother to the new Chinese Bible

---

[1] I was named after my grandfather (who went by his family name, Tom) after he died three weeks before my birth. My mother was influential in leading both of us to the Lord.

[2] The immigration of Chinese women was excluded from 1870-1943 to control the population of Chinese in America. For a survey of these conditions, read Erica Lee, *The Making of Asian America: A History* (New York: Simon & Schuster, 2016).

Church on Wakefield Avenue in order to keep them out of trouble. My grandparents worked long hours with Sunday as their only day of rest, so they did not accompany their children to the church. Although unbelievers, they were extremely grateful to the bus ministry for picking up their children and bringing them home each Sunday. When Chinese Bible Church had special fundraisers or Thanksgiving banquets, Kay Jen and Yun Yee were always eager to participate. They also encouraged their children to attend summer camps because they had no time or money for vacations as a family.

God's Kindness

Kay Jen never practiced the ritual ancestor worship which he believed to be fake, but Yun Yee observed certain cultural customs in order to receive good luck and to appease the demons. Little by little, though, they heard about Jesus as their children brought home gospel literature and sermon cassettes recorded in Chinese. The pastor of the church also made a special effort to befriend Kay Jen and this relationship blossomed when the pastor waited in the hospital while Kay Jen was undergoing surgery. The pastor's unusual show of care broke through my grandfather's reserve and earned his trust. He said it was the first time a white man had ever shown him kindness. My grandfather had made his way in a country greatly prejudiced against Asians and had come to expect nothing good from white people in general. Instead, he insisted it was better to be your own boss in your own business than to serve those who mistreat you. The church's kindness stood out to him in a world of racial hate.

God's Reward

In September 1970, both Kay Jen and Yun Yee accepted Jesus Christ as Lord and Savior. Soon after, both were baptized and began to attend the Chinese Bible Church with their children. My grandmother said that Jesus lifted her burden of appeasing the demons for good luck and my grandfather learned to pass on to others the kindness he had received. Both Kay Jen and Yun Yee Tom were buried at the Mountain View

Cemetery in Oakland. Yet both are also now living with our Lord Jesus Christ and eagerly await their family's arrival (1 Thessalonians 4:13-18).

Questions for Reflection:

1. Why would persons of Chinese descent intentionally choose to gather in a Chinese immigrant church? Do you think Christians today should still gather in ethnic-specific churches?

2. How does a society characterized by overt and covert racism provide the church more opportunities to be light in the darkness? Describe a time when you witnessed certain Christians demonstrating unusual kindness in such a way that people were brought to faith in Jesus.

CHRIST IN THE HOOD
Tom & Anita Borek

Late one night, May phoned us in distress: "Please, call the pastor! My husband, Luke, got drunk and I need someone to come and take away his guns." Our hearts filled with concern as we prayed for a safe intervention and for Luke's response. We also thanked the Lord that May now trusted us enough to seek our help. One year ago, we never could have imagined such a conversation.

Much had changed quickly for us, as so often happens when we give our lives in sacrifice to God (Romans 12:1). We now had a front row seat to the enormity of needs in the urban community where we lived. This served to deepen our trust in Jesus as we surrendered control of our time, resources, and often personal safety for the sake of kingdom ministry.

Christ in Marriage

Serving together as husband and wife also greatly refreshed our marriage. Both of us had become committed followers of Jesus later in life. So we knew the hardships of being self-centered in the past, but also the joy of God's transformation as a married couple committed to Christ. Growing up as good Catholics, we had known that Jesus was sinless and that we were not. No matter how hard we tried, we could never be perfectly righteous. But one day, God opened our eyes to see how Jesus had done everything right, so that we would be made right with him. Jesus came down to perfectly fulfill his Father's will, pay for our sins on the cross, and conquer death through his resurrection (1 Corinthians 15:3-4). This gamechanger took us from feeling like failures to confidently knowing that God counted his Son's perfect righteousness as ours (2 Corinthians 5:21).

Christ on Mission

As we grew in faith, God's Spirit placed the desire in our hearts to serve him for his glory. Our previous motive for volunteering at our children's schools, with community sports, and even the church had been to simply "pay it forward" as we did our part for society. Yet as new Christians, we wanted our service to directly accomplish God's kingdom work. So we started saving up vacation time to go on short-term mission trips which would tremendously impact our spiritual growth. One time, we traveled to the Dominican Republic to support an urban pastor's Vacation Bible School and to build Prefab chapels for rural churches. These experiences reminded us how Jesus had left his home in heaven to live among sinners who needed him as Savior. Jesus came to not only save our souls, but also to show us an example of perfect humility (Philippians 2:3-8). As we continued to serve on missions, our sending church taught us how to love unfamiliar people in uncomfortable circumstances (and there was certainly plenty of both). We chose to embrace each new adventure like a roller coaster that starts off with a scary drop, but ends with an exhilarating, "Let's do it again!" Every time we returned from serving, we were ready to trust the Lord for even greater challenges. We viewed any discomforts as only minor inconveniences compared to Christ coming down for us.

Yet after what turned out to be our final international mission trip, our desire to serve felt strangely different. We still sensed a growing compassion for lost people throughout the world, but we no longer felt the burden to go out again on missions. We were also recent empty nesters with more time and resources than ever before. So we started praying for God's direction: "Where and how are you calling us to serve?"

Christ in the City

We soon received the answer when God directed our hearts to help with an inner-city church plant in Indianapolis. Our home church in the more affluent suburbs had planted Brookside Community Church with a vision to bring gospel care to an urban community from a different cultural and socioeconomic background. As soon as we visited Brookside, we witnessed their significant needs and saw that, in many ways, we would be the minority if we continued to serve with them. The congregants were predominantly African American and lived at a lower income level than the people in our home church. This venture would be cross-cultural missions in our own backyard or, at least, on the other side of town (Isaiah 6:8).

The two of us were no strangers to poverty having both grown up in poorer Polish American families. Yet our family's goal had been to better ourselves through education and then move out of the neighborhood. We also experienced the hurtful nature of discrimination as Poles were often the butt of jokes. Yet as we prepared to serve, God would redeem our painful past by returning us to a life of sacrifice and racial tension for the sake of ministry. Over the years, we would lean in to do the uncomfortable as we witnessed God's faithful presence for our task (Matthew 28:20b).

We first met with the pastor of Brookside and offered to serve regularly. Yet surprisingly, instead of welcoming our help, the pastor told us to go home and pray about our decision for thirty days. He wisely understood how common it was in urban ministry for volunteers to quickly come and go. So we prayed for thirty days and, to the pastor's surprise, returned to the church and threw ourselves into serving. This began the next chapter in our spiritual growth as we attended our suburban church on Saturdays and served in the city on Sundays. Soon, we were also going to the city for mid-week Bible study and coordinating the food pantry as well. We attended city weddings (not enough) and city funerals (too many). We celebrated whenever students completed high school despite the 20% graduation rate and learned to love both churchgoers and their unbelieving neighbors. Worship and discipleship functioned quite differently at Brookside than we were used to. People often came to church appearing less than their best: dirty, drunk, or stoned. Yet they also seemed more transparent in their relationship with the Lord and with each other, singing loudly while clapping or stomping to the tambourine. They spoke honestly about their sin and brokenness as they confessed their need for God (e.g., Luke 18:10-14).

One time, a Brookside friend, Jamie, came with us to an event at our suburban sending church. When Jamie saw the large modern building and expensive cars in the parking lot, she asked, "Do these people even need

Jesus?" We responded, "Oh, Jamie. They need Jesus just as much as people in the hood, but it might take far longer for them to know it" (e.g., Luke 18:18-25). It was surreal bringing Jamie back to the hood that night like being transported to a different planet. As we entered the city, we felt our guard go up against the physical dangers and spiritual warfare which were simply more apparent.

We soon realized that returning to our suburban home, after serving every week, constructed an insurmountable barrier to building close relationships. So we decided to move into the city to live among the people we were serving. Like Christ, in his incarnation, our ministry proved most effective as we shared intimate joys and struggles with our friends and fellow church members. We learned, in small measure, why Christ had come down for us.

On Sundays, many neighborhood children walked for blocks in order to get their bellies and their souls filled up at Brookside. They often came without their parents who did not attend the church. Yet one time, a little girl scraped her knee so badly that we had to bring her home. We weren't concerned until our friend, Jamie, who genuinely loves all kiddos, warned us about the little girl's family: "Those people shot a gun at me last week!" Jamie repeatedly urged us to be careful and even went with us just in case. We met the little girl's momma at the door and explained how the church had loved and cared for her daughter. Then, to Jamie's surprise, that momma's face filled with joy and thanked us for our efforts. Jamie's faith blossomed as she spoke about loving this little girl the way Jesus loves us even when others may try to harm us.

Jamie was also one of the few friends from Brookside who visited our suburban home. She witnessed the earthly comforts we had given up in order to live in the hood and lent us her street cred to help us minister to others as we gained the trust of our community. She also gently showed us how to use fewer and simpler words when teaching and exhorting others. We learned that a typical vocabulary for Brookside was about 300 words, whereas many suburbanites used 700 words or more. In time, Jamie observed how we grew in faith because we had chosen to give up so much.

Friends often ask whether we would embark on this adventure if we could do it all over again and we always answer, "ABSOLUTELY, YES!" Every step of faith during those nine years of ministry greatly expanded our understanding of God's power and his faithfulness. Our family learned much about God's radical love through that experience of trusting him in the city. Though, at times, it had been dangerous and often uncomfortable, the One who counts the hairs on our head and knows the number of our days had equipped us to serve him by his will and for his glory.

Christ in Us

May's husband, Luke, would eventually change. He was broken by his sin and willingly gave up his guns. Those guns then remained hidden beneath our bed for many months while Luke was being discipled in the Scriptures. Luke and May themselves spent a great deal of time in our home hearing how God had transformed us both personally and in our marriage. These conversations only happened, though, because we had moved into the hood and we only moved into the hood because Christ first came to us. "In this the love of God was made manifest among us, that God sent his only Son into the world, so that we might live through him" (1 John 4:9).

Questions for Reflection:

1. What concerns would you have about moving into the most dangerous or impoverished section of your city? How does geography play a part in establishing social and financial capital? What would you need to change about your life if God called you to such a ministry?

2. What did Jesus give up to move into our hood (Philippians 2:5-8)? How can you practically model his loving sacrifice and selfless humility in your relationships with others (vv. 3-4)?

MORE THAN LUCK
Habtamu Sisay

I know about Camel, Marlboro, and Newport from working the counter at a gas station convenience store in Boston, Massachusetts. It was my first job in America as a 23-year-old immigrant from Ethiopia. I also learned how to pump gas and check engine oil in that full-service station before I ever owned a car. Many travelers passed me by as they journeyed up-and-down the eastern seaboard, but I myself wasn't headed anywhere without the proper papers. So I am grateful to the Reverend Michael E. Haynes, whose organization helped me get a student visa. I am grateful to this country which granted me asylum and opened the door for my permanent residence status. I received many opportunities through which I was able to continue my education, find a better job, and travel freely without fear. When I purchased my first home, I felt I had accomplished the American dream.

This and lots of other things had to go right for me before I had to realize how wrong I'd been.

Village Hospitality

Growing up, my family in Ethiopia had been very poor, but the challenges of poverty taught me to be a survivor as I was expected to contribute to my family's well-being from an early age. We lived on the outskirts of the capital, Addis Ababa, in a village which the main roads had not yet reached. So as a child of eight or nine, I would listen for the delivery trucks to honk their horns. My friends and I would then run to the edge of our village, lift the heavy crates of Coca-Cola bottles onto our heads, and deliver them to the village shops for five cents a case. The first time I tried to carry one, I dropped all twenty-four bottles and broke quite a few. In order to provide for my family, I also polished shoes for local businessmen, cared for the sheep and goats on our family farm, and climbed trees to collect firewood for my mother.

28

Our family's poverty and lack of connections made it extremely unlikely that I would ever make it to America on my own. Even now, I'm still amazed that I am living in this country with all of its privileges and opportunities. In the past, I considered my journey to America as a lucky strike and nothing more. But since then, I have seen God's providence in all of it (Acts 17:26). The Lord prompted a generous man, Dr. Ralph Wolf, as an instrument of his grace to open up endless avenues which would not have been available had I remained in Ethiopia.

Tech Support

At the forefront of these many blessings, was meeting my wife, Yewbdar. We met while I was working in Boston for an IT company—she needed help setting up her computer and I was just the right man for the job. We spoke the same dialect, shared a similar culture, and strongly desired the well-being of the Ethiopian people. In our home country, many had lived in peace for quite some time. So despite our spotted history of civil wars and senseless killings, my wife and I grew up in a cultural environment with fairly little conflict.

Since then, however, tribal animosities have escalated in our homeland, causing many to lose their lives, their generational wealth, and their daily peace of mind. My people can no longer move about freely and work in certain parts of the country. Neighbors have grown suspicious of one another and even churches have become victims of such ethnic division that they do not speak about the peace of Christ (Romans 5:1). Our hearts ache over the tribalism among our people because we know that the sinful pride at the root of this problem goes much deeper than our skin color. In Ethiopia, all of us are black. So our struggle arises not from racial strife or the merits of our melanin, but from our sinful hearts (Jeremiah 13:23). The final solution, therefore, is not merely political action or social justice, but rather the grace of Christ which guards us from following the selfish desires of our flesh (Ephesians 2:1-3).

As unified as my wife and I were in our love for the Ethiopian people and our concern for the struggles they were going through, I wasn't able to see that our marriage was crumbling because of my own sin.

Saving Grace

I was baptized in an Ethiopian evangelical church in 1992. Yet at the time, I had no idea what it truly meant to be a Christian. I never took the initiative to study God's Word for myself and I loved my sin so much that I turned away from God. I didn't think that he could ever change my life. Yet on January 28, 2013, I came home from work and found my wife had left me. She and our two young boys were gone without a warning or even a note. I was unable to connect with them or to find out where they were. A few days later, though, I was called into court and served with a restraining order. According to the law, I was forbidden from seeing or speaking with my wife and children for an entire year.

I was so broken by the shock that I began to pray as an act of desperation. I had nowhere else to turn, but to the God in whom I had once professed my faith. Then, as I prayed, the Lord confronted me about my rejection of his love and my selfishness as a husband and a father. I realized what a fool I'd been, trying to provide security for my family through human means. In my pride, I had torn apart my family. I couldn't sleep. I couldn't eat. I couldn't work. I cried for over a week as I begged the Lord to forgive me. Finally, in that empty home, I received God's grace and a renewed desire in my heart to know his Word. I went to Panera Bread every day and read my Bible for hours at a time. When I couldn't sleep, I downloaded more than 3,000 sermons from a pastor in Los Angeles named John MacArthur and listened to them all night. God used my brokenness to make me a different person and a follower of Jesus as I surrendered my life to Christ.

My wife, meanwhile, had taken our boys to North Carolina, where she lived for ten months with the help of some friends. She made no contact with me, but the Lord was graciously working to change her heart as well. She providentially spoke with Pastor Abebayehu, an Ethiopian marriage counselor in Minnesota who counseled her by phone about our marriage. He then proceeded to contact Pastor Miheretu in Boston to help the two of us reconcile. So, ten months after my wife had left me for good, I drove down to North Carolina to see her again with our two boys. Pastor Abebayehu met us there to help us make peace and to bring healing to our marriage. In tears, my wife and I mutually agreed to break the restraining order and we all drove back home together as a reunited family. By the works of the law, there is no reason Yewbdar and I should be happily married today. Though we had come from the same tribe with a similar cultural background, we still managed to grievously sin against each other. Yet by the grace of God, we are still together and, to our surprise, preparing for ministry. God, by his grace, used friends in our Ethiopian evangelical community, an American pastor in California I had never met, and the invisible hand of his divine grace to restore what we could not.

Our Return Home

Since then, our desire to return home has continued to grow within us. Yewbdar and I hope to plant a church in Addis Ababa which will reach the lost and train workers for Christ's church. Our people must know the one, true God as he has revealed himself in Scripture and not in traditions alone. They must know him as the only one who promises true justice and peace. So we desire to teach our people these biblical truths that they might have a personal relationship with God, experience his forgiveness of sins, and become his children through believing faith in Jesus Christ.

My wife and I have grown more certain of this calling after a recent vision trip encouraged us with God's answers to our prayers. We had prayed that God would allow us to start a Bible study in my home village and also to provide a man to lead the study after we returned from our trip. God then answered our prayers by introducing us to a brother who had come to faith while training as an orthodox priest. He agreed to help us carry on the Bible study without a moment's hesitation because he loves to study God's Word and has worked quite hard to reach others like himself with their background in religious legalism. Through this man's bold witness, many have heard the gospel and now experience new freedom through faith in Christ alone. It has been refreshing and encouraging for us to partner for the sake of the gospel and we pray that connections like these will bear much fruit for the glory of God and the good of our people.

My wife and I are eager to return now that we have seen and experienced the great need and tremendous promise of ministry in Ethiopia. Since we already know the language and the culture, we can fit in better than missionaries who begin as outsiders. Our future return will also provide a built-in testimony for anyone asking why we would give up a life of comfort in America. In addition, my ministry training in the U.S. will stretch much further in Ethiopia where many pastors do not have formal theological education. There is a growing hunger among my people to receive the gospel and to grow in the Christian faith. So, at such a time as this, what they need the most is Christ (Romans 15:20-21).

Questions for Reflection:

1. Do you notice or speak to the convenience store clerks or the gas station attendants in your life? How would you treat them differently if you looked at them as either a fellow believer or a lost person in need of Christ?

2. In what ways are Christians called to minister cross-culturally either in our local communities or through global missions? In what ways should we strategically make use of our social, linguistic, and cultural familiarities?

LOVE HEALS ALL WOUNDS
Joe Toledo

I grew up in Los Angeles, California, with sixteen aunts and uncles who were all quite proud to be Mexican. My earliest memories were of them reminding me, "Joe, you are not Hispanic, or Latino, or even Mexican American. Your family came from Mexico, therefore you are Mexican and should be proud to be a Mexican." My family made sure that being Mexican remained essential to my identity.

A Broken Family

My first real experience of racism came surprisingly from my mother. Her parents had been Mexican immigrants, but she had grown up in El Paso, Texas before marrying my father who had come from Mexico at the age of seventeen. My parents divorced when I was only eight years old, but I remember mom always telling me stories about dad's deadbeat brothers and deadbeat friends: "All they want to do is come over to barbecue and drink beer on the weekends. Your father would rather play the big man and feed all his buddies than pay our rent." My mom planted many negative thoughts in my head about all Mexican men being lazy and good for nothing. She also hated having to interpret for Mexicans who had lived in this country for years, but had never learned how to speak English. She would call them stupid and lazy. My mom was proud to be Mexican, but she believed that laziness would get you nowhere in life.

I still have fond childhood memories, however, of visiting my extended family in Mexico. We would stay at my uncle's motel in Ensenada, The Motel of the Sun. Everything was free and we had a lot of fun on those trips. My other uncles owned entire blocks on Ensenada's main street where many people still respected their family. They were the lucky ones who had managed to hold onto their wealth, even when many other family members had lost everything after the Mexican revolution (c. 1920).

My father's parents had been among those who were not so fortunate

34

when they immigrated to the United States with virtually nothing.[1] They had to rebuild their lives out of poverty with hard work and a lot of perseverance. My dad and his brothers also faced the cruelty of racism from the sailors stationed at San Pedro. He and my uncles would reminisce about fights they got into for moving in on non-Mexican women and dating them. These difficult circumstances, however, taught them how to stand up for themselves and to remain proud of their Mexican heritage.

Valley Times

Growing up, I personally experienced very little racism and enjoyed a carefree childhood. I grew up on 9th and Figueroa at the present site of the Los Angeles Convention Center where my sister and I ran wild on the streets and got into all kinds of trouble. The community was mainly Mexican American at the time, so our family fit right in. I would have attended Berrendo Junior High and Fremont High School, until my mom decided to move us from downtown Los Angeles to the San Fernando Valley. Her desire, as a single mom, to give her children a better life was one of the most significant changes for our family. My mom worked as a seamstress for a well-known company called Rosemary Reed which made women's sportswear and bathing suits. So when the company moved to the Valley, they offered to relocate my mom as well. That move completely changed the direction my life was headed. I probably would have ended up in a Hispanic gang if we had stayed in the city, but instead I received the chance of a better life in the Valley. My mother taught me, by her courageous decision, to take pride in myself and to work hard for whatever I wanted to accomplish. Nothing would simply be handed to me. We were so poor that, some days, my mother would send my sister and I to collect a certain kind of weed that grew in the sidewalk cracks. Then she would boil

---

[1] My father and his siblings were considered U.S. citizens because his mother had crossed the border and stayed with family in America to birth each of her children. This practice of "birth tourism" was a common industry back then and is still a practice for many today.

those greens to supplement our dinner. I later passed on these values I had learned to my own children that no matter what choices they made in life, they should always work hard and strive to be the best at whatever they did.

When we moved, my mom bought us a home in the Valley for about $11,000. I attended Birmingham for both Junior High and High School where I met Sharron, my future wife. In God's providence, my mother's earthly desire for a better life led me to Sharron who in turn led me to Jesus. Sharron was a straight-A student, a born-again Christian, and much different from all the girls I had dated before. Any parent would have been very proud to have Sharron as a daughter. Yet one of the first questions my mom asked me was, "Do her parents know that you are Mexican?" She would ask this question over and over even though I couldn't understand why. My attitude was, "What difference does it make that Sharron is white?" I soon found out the significance in eleventh grade when Sharron's parents finally learned that I was Mexican. Suddenly, she was not allowed to date me at all, so we had to sneak around instead. One of our non-Hispanic friends would ask Sharron out and pick her up for the date, then we would all go out as a group. Sharron and I would end up together by the end of the night, but it seemed strange to me that we needed all these creative measures just because I was Mexican.

Big Tent Revival

I also got to be with Sharron when she invited me to her youth group at St. Mark's Episcopal Church. So I went, not because I was interested in Jesus, but because I was interested in Sharron. But then, one day, the youth director took us all to an Oral Roberts tent revival at Devonshire Downs where the Cal State Northridge dorms have since been built. Oral Roberts was a hell-and-brimstone evangelist who shouted and screamed a lot about how sinners would burn in hell. At any of his tent revivals, you could watch crazy people rushing forward, crying, "Save me! Save me!" I had no desire to attend except to be entertained by all those crazies. Yet before I knew what had happened, the Lord touched my heart at that revival. I found myself sobbing as I walked to the altar and accepted Jesus as my Lord and Savior. Sharron herself led me in the prayer and my life began to change as I gradually realized the significance of my decision.

The Stone Age

During our senior year of high school, my relationship with Sharron also changed from boyfriend and girlfriend to truly being in love. I asked her to marry me after we both attended and graduated from college. Yet this is when I first realized how much hatred and anger exists because of racism. Such sinful prejudice could even destroy a loving family. Sharron was a good Christian daughter, a hard-working student, and the valedictorian of her high school class. Yet none of that mattered to her parents who were ready to throw her out of their home and cut her off from the family because she fell in love with someone of a different race. Their hatred ran so deep that they refused to let a Mexican join their family. They felt that, if we married, our children would never quite fit in and be considered half-breeds. So Sharron was forced to choose between them and me. This decision was very hard for her as she wrestled with God's command to honor her father and mother, while still following what she believed to be God's will for us. Thankfully, she chose to marry me and has continued to honor the Lord through our sixty-plus years together.

After her decision, though, Sharron's parents told her to pack up her belongings and move out of the house. So, instead of going to college, we chose to get married right away. That anger and bitterness between our two families continued throughout our first three years of marriage and reminded me of my mother's concern that some people would reject us simply on the basis of race or culture. My parents, for their part, loved Sharron as a member of our family. Everyone adored her, including all my aunts and uncles. Yet Sharron's family kept their distance until it felt like a big stone stood between her parents and me. In fact, I remember telling Sharron's mother during one particular argument, that she was still living in the stone age. So, to spite me, they placed a large stone on their fireplace mantel and called it "the stone age." This pettiness came from a supposedly

Christian family, yet the Lord still had plans for all of us. Sharron and I began teaching God's Word in her former youth group at St. Mark's. And since her parents also attended the church, we had to forge an uneasy truce for several years.

The God Who Speaks

Then one day, God called us to serve in what is now New Life Church in Woodland Hills and I was given the opportunity to preach a farewell message for the congregation of St. Mark's. I cried the entire time I was speaking, but somewhere in the middle of the sermon I heard God tell me to give an altar call. I ignored it at first because ours was not the kind of church to do that, but God continued to press this burden on my heart. I didn't know what else to do, so I listened to God's voice and called for people to come to the front during my closing prayer. When I opened my eyes, I saw only five people still sitting in their seats, while everyone else had come forward to the altar. So then, I asked the Lord, "What do I do now? This was your idea in the first place." I spoke a few more words which I can't now recall, but I know that God's Holy Spirit touched many people that day. The Lord even miraculously broke down the hatred between me and my in-laws. We stopped hating each other as we submitted to God's Word, then we watched him heal our family. Sharron's parents, who had been in the congregation that day, came forward to commit their lives to Christ. We forgave each other and our family was instantly healed like no division had ever existed. God placed his ointment upon a wound that had been festering for over three years.

This forgiveness between us also unleashed the flow of the Holy Spirit's work in the rest of our family. As time passed, my sister and her family came to know the Lord. Sharron's sister then followed Jesus and began to serve in ministry. Since our marriage, the seed of the gospel has led to over one hundred family members and extended family members believing in Christ as well. They came to know and love our Lord Jesus Christ because my faithful wife had known and loved a brash, young Mexican boy.

Together, with God's help and direction, Sharron and I also raised our family in the Lord. Our painful experience compelled us to teach our children to respect people from every race. We are now proud to claim a family of mixed heritage and trust that our story of God working through the hatred and ugliness of racism has laid a foundation for generations to come. The Lord has shown me through his Word, through life experiences, and through my marriage to Sharron that he is always with us. He has never failed us and works all things together for good as we listen to his voice and seek his guidance. God has restored what hatred tried to destroy. God's love has healed our wounds (Psalm 147:3).

Questions for Reflection:

1. How would you respond if your parents or close relatives objected strongly to your marrying someone of a different ethnicity? Would you break fellowship with them over this issue?

2. In the church, God forms a family out of strangers. How does "the Golden Rule" and the teachings of Jesus (Matthew 7:12; Mark 3:35; Luke 14:26) shape your understanding of family relationships in the church and in your home?

TO CROSS AN OCEAN
Amanda Sugimura

I screamed as the man jabbed a needle in my head, but the painful shock meant I was still alive. Only moments before, my infant body had fallen limp and like so many babies in the camp, my heart then stopped from beating. I'd been a sickly child ever since my mother's milk dried up, though there wasn't much for her to do. We were clustered in a Malaysian refugee camp called Cherating. Refugees crowded into shanty towns several stories high, constructed from salvaged timbers, corrugated metal, and walls made of plastic sheets. The conditions were filthy as rainstorms sent floods of contaminated water sweeping through the camp such that many contracted diseases like hepatitis or malaria. We lived on instant noodles and any fish the men could catch, but most days we went without.

Becoming Boat People

My family lost our home in 1979 when civil war forced us to flee from the humble fishing village of Cà Mau. It seemed the entire country was tipping toward our southern end like rats from a sinking ship. Frightened refugees piled onto flimsy vessels not fit for ocean voyage and many of those boats capsized in the waves or were seized by marauding pirates. The few who slipped past danger then dumped their human cargo into makeshift camps in Southeast Asia. So we were happy just to be alive.

Vietnam has historically been a battleground for the Chinese, French, and, in those days, the Communists. Yet in 1973, when the U.S. found they couldn't win the war, they pulled out troops and left our country in massive chaos. Navy officers like my father, who had risked their lives assisting U.S. forces, were put to death (or worse) by the Viet Cong. Many of my father's friends had already been imprisoned and tortured for information in the re-education camps. Yet when our family fled the country with a boatload of others, it was my dad who bravely piloted our vessel to freedom across the churning sea.

Crossing the World

We survived in Cherating for about a year until my parents' sponsorship to America became their ticket out. We had been willing to go to the first country which made room for us, but we secretly hoped for the U.S.A. since a few of our relatives had already gone ahead. America was a promised land of incredible wealth and opportunity. Yet of all the places in this vast country, we were placed in a crime-ridden section of Oakland, California, with its corner liquor stores and iron bars on every window. Our family moved into a dingy yellow building with many other aunties and uncles and we lived near Lake Merritt before the city cleaned it up. Dilapidated homes peeked out behind double-barricaded fences, vicious guard dogs barked throughout the night, and side streets boasted of drug deals and gang activity. My immigrant parents taught me how to live in fear and to always watch my back to keep from being followed.

Both of my parents worked long hours and often left my brother and myself alone. Mom attended night school to open a donut shop, but the work seemed very hard for not much profit (and she also ate too many donuts). She then became a seamstress and found contract work sewing wedding dresses for well-off brides. Her skill set brought in jobs for many other immigrants, but the work was hard on her hands and eyes. Dad delivered newspapers up-and-down the Oakland hills. Every morning, he woke up early to prepare his load, then walked the route because he didn't own a car. At the end of every month, he collected fees from house-to-house (in those days before e-payments) only to have some clients refuse to pay because they knew they could. Years later, he and some friends would open up a phở restaurant, which created many jobs for others. My parents worked hard because they were too proud to stay on welfare. They rarely spent money on themselves, but were always generous toward those with less.

As immigrants, we kept mostly to our own people: Chinese and Vietnamese. I attended preschool in Oakland Chinatown where I met my best friend, Winnie, and I don't remember any social gatherings except

41

with family. In our experience, the wealthy people with business connections were always white, so we had to stay in their good graces. Yet the criminals we knew were black, so we avoided them. Six times, we were robbed (twice at gunpoint) and always by a black man. We didn't necessarily hate black people, but we feared them because we could not tell which ones would do us harm. My mother called them *haakgwai*, "black ghosts" and we kept our distance as much as possible.

Finding Home

My parents provided us a home, then also gave an unexpected gift when they sent us to the newly-chartered Chinese Christian Schools which offered daily busing for immigrant kids like us. In that school, I first learned English and I also gave my life to Jesus. I loved learning more and more about the Bible and the world around me, but I did not realize how sheltered I had become. Our daily bus served as a haven to whisk me away from the darkness in my neighborhood to a place where mostly everyone looked like me. Yet over time, I began to notice the world outside those windows and grew self-conscious while riding on those busses that declared in big, block letters: "CHINESE CHRISTIAN SCHOOLS." What do others think when they see our bus? Do they look at us as different? I dreamed at night about white kids making "slant eyes" through the window or yelling out, "Go back to China!" No one seemed to notice if a group of white kids or black kids traveled on a bus together. Yet people treated Asians as perpetual outsiders even though most of us had grown up in this country. It became easier just to keep to ourselves, which only added to our foreignness.

It was not until attending the University of the Pacific that I broke out of my Asian bubble. My engineering cohort gave me reason to belong in the majority white culture and my InterVarsity Christian Fellowship brought together students from all different backgrounds and ethnicities. I fit in well because I'd been adapting all my life, but this accommodation seemed to only go one way. I would never dare to invite my white friends to my Chinese church back home. What would they think of us? Would they feel uncomfortable in the minority? The more I assimilated into the dominant culture, the less I felt at home in mine.

I now attend a multiethnic church where my husband is the pastor. It is a place where pockets of Asians might speak Chinese, Tagalog, Hindi, or Korean. Yet all of us worship together in English and half of our congregation is not even Asian. Cultural factors have taken a backseat to our shared identity in Jesus Christ. We can invite non-Asian friends and neighbors to this church without fear of their discomfort because we enjoy a sense of deep belonging despite our many differences. Even today, my upbringing might still shape my view of race, my desire to fit in, and the insecurity of my foreignness. Yet the experience of God's grace has allowed me to see all people through his eyes as we form a place called home.

Questions for Reflection:

1. What are some various reasons people immigrate to another country? What would cause them to seek refuge or asylum? How can you minister to them cross-culturally just as you would on the global mission field?

2. Why are certain minorities treated like perpetual foreigners? In what ways are different minorities often set against each other for the benefit of the dominant culture?

STUCK BETWEEN BLACK AND WHITE
Gary Alaka

Growing up, I was convinced there were only three black people in Bulgaria: me, my brother, and my sister. I knew this wasn't the case, but it might as well have been since Eastern Europe isn't exactly a mecca of diversity. Our family lived in a small community surrounded by relatives and friends, so our interaction with "strangers" was fairly limited. Most Bulgarians who approached us thought we were African tourists and tried to communicate with us in broken English. My favorite joke was responding to them in fluent Bulgarian and watch them walk away with astonishment on their face. Our family looked different than others, but that never really bothered me as a child.

The Space Between

My experience of race did not begin to "define who I was" until our family moved to the United States. Up until that point, I hadn't thought too much about race. I was still young and race wasn't really discussed at home. Yet as I began to assimilate into American culture, my "otherness" began to reveal itself in small and seemingly innocent ways. Being bi-racial (half-Nigerian and half-Armenian) meant I didn't quite fit into either world, while also giving me unprecedented access to both. Externally, I appeared black, which formed most people's first impression. They would see the color of my skin and make up their minds before I ever spoke a word. Internally, though, I felt and thought like an Armenian. My parents had split up when I was five, so my mother raised me with Armenian customs and traditions. We spoke Armenian at home and ate their food.

Being a newcomer to this country, I had to re-learn English alongside other recent immigrants. I was a quick learner, though, and befriended my classmates by translating assignments for them and helping them get connected at school. These peers should have naturally become my circle of friends, but they never fully accepted me as belonging because I was too dark to be Armenian and too different to be black. So I often remained just "a fly on the wall" who observed the interactions of both groups. I laughed politely, but nervously, along with others to make them feel at ease. Yet I was still trying to figure out who I was in a world that constantly bombarded me with various options and ideas.

Backhanded Compliments

My most memorable experiences with covert racism were the backhanded compliments not intended to harm. For example, adults I should have looked up to such as teachers, counselors, and coaches, often told me, "You're so well spoken." The shocked amazement in their voices revealed how little they expected of me based on the color of my skin and the entrenched assumptions in their hearts. Yet instead of seeing their prejudice for what it was, I began to wear it as a badge of honor. I resolved to overcome those perceived biological limitations and to shine brightly in a sea of darkness. The insidious problem of racism has so deeply permeated our society that both perpetrators and victims will succumb to its lies (Titus 3:3).

As I grew older, unintentional racism took on different forms. Schoolwork always came easy for me. So I hoped my grades would not only grant me acceptance into college, but also provide some much-needed financial aid. By God's grace, I received an invitation to attend Loyola Marymount University which even waived the application fee. I had never even heard of the school. So I was shocked when they not only accepted me, but also offered a sizable scholarship. LMU is a costly private university which my family could never have afforded without assistance.

This reality, however, also resulted in a certain prejudice. As I walked around on campus, I cannot count the number of people who assumed I had received an athletic scholarship instead of an academic one. Although LMU sports had not been relevant since the 1989 March Madness tournament, strangers often asked me which team I played on almost immediately after I met them. This seemingly innocent question was grounded in the assumption that I could only afford the college because of an athletic scholarship—unintentional racism. Many people made these comments without even recognizing their bias.

Restoration Piece

After graduation, I began to wrestle with life's existential questions. As I viewed the world through a bi-racial lens, I placed all of humanity in only two buckets: white and not-white. The first group was not inherently better than the other, but it sure seemed to have all the advantages. My worldview was further reinforced by people's comments equating my positive traits to "whiteness" and my negative traits to "blackness." Being "white" meant being "good," although being "good" was never good enough. As I constantly sought the approval of those around me, I did everything in my power to earn their affirmation. Then, although I did not realize it at the time, that mentality also manifested itself in how I assumed God saw me: a stained canvas needing a fresh coat of paint. Stroke-by-stroke I would lean into my "whiteness," trying to whitewash the parts I assumed were "bad."

One day, however, through the intentional ministry of friends God had placed in my life, I began to see myself through his eyes as a sinner desperately in need of salvation. My solution was no longer "whiteness," but rather holiness through the blood of Christ. For the first time, my "otherness" no longer defined me. Instead, my new identity unified me as "one in Christ Jesus" with every believer in the church (Galatians 3:28).

Adding to the Mix

The church today is still far from perfect. When I began to date my now-wife almost ten years ago, her Chinese ethnicity took a major role in our relationship. We knew that interracial marriage would have its difficulties, but we trusted that our unity in Christ would keep us grounded. My wife's Asian heritage also meant we had to address some unspoken assumptions in her family, but by God's grace we overcame our fears and pursued peace in our extended family.

Now, as a father, I look with wonder on our newborn son and consider what hope his future holds. What ethnic identity will he experience as he grows into a man? What conversations will we have about race? I hope he will see himself first and foremost as a child of God though the world may define him otherwise.

Ten years later, I thank the Lord to be surrounded by brothers and sisters in the church who see me for more than just the color of my skin. These men and women know me inside-and-out, entrust me to lead their children in youth ministry, and refuse to shy away from difficult conversations. We still have a long way to go in society and in the church, but I am confident in Christ that the work is worth the effort.

Questions for Reflection:

1. Have you ever felt stuck in-between two distinct cultures? What makes these halfway experiences so hard to navigate? In what ways do you naturally "code-switch" when you find yourself in different cultural settings?

2. Clarify the difference between overt (intentional) and covert (unintended) racism. Why does God count you guilty for unintentional sins of ignorance even if you did not mean to offend (e.g., Leviticus 4; Numbers 15)?

ARRANGED BY GOD
Thiru Rajeswaran

I grew up in a small town in Tamil Nadu to a family of Hindu faith. My mother and her parents labored in the field as farmhands, while my father was often away from home to look for work. Like most Indian families, we celebrated cultural events such as the Festival of Lights (*Diwali*), Tamil New Year (*Puthandu*), India Independence Day, and other religious holidays. We enjoyed games like cricket and ate our favorite foods of *idli* and *dosa* for breakfast with *sambar* and coconut chutney. For lunch and dinner, we often enjoyed rice and curry with the occasional *rasam* or curd. I had a pleasant childhood though I did not know the Lord. My parents only called upon their god in times of need and did not regularly worship in the temple or at home.

Encountering the Cross

By God's grace, I was fortunate to study in a Christian school from the first to the eighth grade. We learned our studies in Tamil with English as a secondary language. Most of our teachers claimed to be Christians, but I do not remember that they ever taught us the Bible. I only recall that one of the classrooms displayed a large picture of Jesus hanging crucified as blood dripped from the nails in his hands and feet and from the crown of thorns upon his head. Although I attended a Christian school, I never even saw a Bible until my twelfth-grade year. Only then did I learn of what Jesus Christ had done for me by his death upon the cross. Throughout my childhood, there was also not a single Christian church in town.

Accepting the Invitation

After completing my secondary education, I moved 500 kilometers away to attend a college in the crowded city of Chennai. I stayed in a women's hostel where I worked, studied, and commuted to school. This was my first time living on my own and I was very homesick at first. Those were painful days filled with new faces and a deep longing for the

48

familiarities of home. In that guest house, though, I met an older grandma who was staying in the room next door. (I never learned why she was there since she was neither a student nor a working woman.) Late one evening, she asked me to accompany her to a New Year's watchnight service at her church and I answered, "Yes," without quite knowing what it was all about. I went with her to the New Life Assemblies of God Church and for the first time in my life had the wonderful experience of seeing Christians praise the Lord and listen expectantly to his Word.

Soon after, I began attending the Rose of Sharon Assemblies of God Church which was closer to where I lived. I could not initially understand what was preached in the sermons or written in the Bible, but every week I discovered new mercies to strengthen and comfort me from God's Word:

- I am with you always (Matthew 28:20).
- I never leave you nor forsake you (Hebrews 13:5).
- I have called you by name and you are mine. You are very precious to me (Isaiah 43:1, 4).
- I am your present help in times of trouble (Psalm 46:1).
- As a father carries his child and a mother comforts her son, so I will carry and comfort you (Deuteronomy 1:31; Isaiah 66:13).
- I am the Way, the Truth, and the Life (John 14:6).

Embracing New Life

I soon began to read the Bible on my own and committed myself to the Lord in Christian baptism. From that moment on, I decided to follow Jesus Christ as a new creation though still surrounded by my Hindu community. My parents told me to stop attending church because they were ashamed when relatives asked why their daughter was not worshiping the same god as the rest of the family. Their idle threats, however, did not keep me from following Jesus (Luke 14:26-27).

The first major challenge to my faith came in the form of a marriage proposal. My parents, who had been searching for a Hindu groom, had found a man who seemed a suitable match for me. I was bold enough, however, to tell them that I would never stop attending the Christian church or worshiping the living God who had accepted me as his child. My parents did not fully understand my convictions, but they accepted my decision to only marry a Christian man (2 Corinthians 6:14-15).

Trusting God's Arrangements

After I moved to the U.S., a common friend introduced me to my future husband, Chinnadurai. Our two families in India met to arrange the marriage, so I did not meet Chinna in person until just before our wedding. Before that blessed day in 2009, we had only ever spoken over the phone. Yet I know our marriage was arranged by God since I was the first in my family to follow Jesus and my husband was the first in his family as well. As King David wrote in Psalm 9:10, "Those who know your name put their trust in you, for you, O LORD, have not forsaken those who seek you."

Despite the diversity of Los Angeles, my appearance and my culture might still seem strange to some. At the workplace, my Indian accent can also make it hard to communicate and my Christian faith is sometimes despised. Even as I write these words, I am required to work in Canada due to visa regulations, separated from my husband in America. Yet by God's grace, he grants me the wisdom and strength to do my work for the sake of his glory (Colossians 3:23). He has fashioned me through the countless blessings I have received in Christ, especially the peace, hope, and joy that no one else can give or take away. I thank Jesus for all that he has done for me and prayerfully desire to live a life worthy of his calling.

Questions for Reflection:

1. How have changes or crises in your life become ideal moments for the Lord to change your heart? Trace the path of your own spiritual growth on the timeline of God's providence.

2. Do you believe God sovereignly arranges every event in your life? How do you explain when hard things happen?

WHEN GOD PICKS A LAWYER
Fred Voigtmann

The line seemed to stretch for miles as we waited eagerly for the first McDonald's in Taipei to open. Before that life-altering day in 1984, my father could only deliver lukewarm cheeseburgers and fries from the McDonald's in Hong Kong, about an hour's plane ride from Taipei. On one such return flight, as he found his seat, his "fast food" carry-on attracted great demand when another American offered, "I'll give you fifty bucks for that bag!" Apparently, the other passenger had smelled the signature aroma of the Golden Arches wafting from the paper sack my father clutched tightly in both hands. My dad refused him, though, without even wavering in his resolve: *"No way! If I don't come back with this bag for my family, they won't even let me in the door."* Many of those familiar American foods, whether healthy or not, were simply unavailable in Taiwan. We had to relish, so to speak, the smaller things in life.

Stranger in a Strange Land

I was raised in Taipei, Taiwan—first as a military brat, then as a missionary one. So having experienced two different sides of expatriate living, I knew how it felt to be a stranger in a strange land. During our family's travels through Asia in the early 1970's, people were fascinated by the whiteness of our skin. Strangers even came up to touch our fair-colored hair—not in a mean way, but because they had never seen a "foreigner" up close.

My father served two tours in Taiwan with the U.S. military. Then after his second tour and more than a decade of military service, the Lord called my parents to serve as missionaries in Taiwan. After that transition, our family life changed dramatically. We joined the missionary community and left the security of a comfortable salary, base benefits, and familiar hangouts. The military bases where we used to shop, dine, and watch American movies became inaccessible to us once they were handed over to

52

the Taiwanese military in 1979.

To make ends meet, my father began to represent expats in our community who needed legal counsel. His training as a lawyer and his connections with both the Taiwanese military and the police brought him many clients. At first, he worked *pro bono*, but eventually collected legal fees for his services which were often related to immigration. His work of representing clients financially allowed us to remain in Taiwan. My father also served for many years in prison ministry, mostly to American, Canadian, and Australian expats locked up for possession of marijuana. Each sentence could last up to seven years and revealed the hardship of living as foreigners in Taiwan. As early as the tenth grade, I remember seeing those young men's faces behind the security plexiglass as we brought them meager gifts at Christmastime or personal care items. I was transfixed by their pained expressions as we prayed with them about their struggles. Those unforgettable experiences, however, prepared me for my present work with immigrants detained for various reasons such as visa overstay, drug trafficking, or domestic violence. I was blessed with a godly father who modeled how an immigration lawyer should care about his clients and respond compassionately to their trials.

His Choice; My Choice

Once I graduated from high school, I prepared to leave one home in Taiwan and return to another in America. At the time, I never dreamed of becoming a lawyer, much less an immigration lawyer. In fact, "my choice" was to become a doctor. Yet although "the heart of a man plans his way, . . . the Lord establishes his steps" (Proverbs 16:9). When I was accepted into the Pre-Med program at The Ohio State University, I was sure I would become a doctor. When I began to fail organic chemistry the following year, I was sure that I would not.

Getting married in 1987 and transferring to an English major set me on a wonderful path for which I now thank the Lord. I attended law school like my father (though I still didn't want to work with immigrants). Yet as I scoured Ohio to find a job after graduation, my father mentioned he could use my help with his numerous cases in Taiwan.

My wife and I talked and prayed about moving back to accept my father's "job offer" to become an immigration lawyer. We decided to trust God in this step of faith and spent the next four years in Taiwan where the Lord shaped us through both the joys and heartaches of ministry. In 1997, we ended the partnership with my father and moved to Los Angeles with our young family and an uncertain job situation. We encountered many new experiences with church, friends, and, of course, culture. Yet since that day, I have been able to help clients walk through the complicated immigration processes here in America. I never chose to become an immigration lawyer any more than my father had, but God chose that career for both of us (and now for my son as well who has followed in our steps).

Anchor in the Storm

As Christians, every aspect of our life must reflect our faith. We should not be one person on Sunday who plays the part of a Christian, while acting contrary to our identity from Monday to Saturday. I am therefore a Christian who happens to be an immigration lawyer and not the other way around. My faith in God and in his Word directs my every interaction with clients or with U.S. government agencies.

My faith also helps me in my various roles not only as an advocate for my clients before the government, but also as a counselor and confidante who bears their burdens as we navigate the process together. My hope in God remains my anchor as I listen to their stories of suffering on a weekly basis (Hebrews 6:19). I may not always pray *with* my clients (though I do when there is opportunity), but I always pray *for* them. Then, as I speak forth words of hope into their lives, I reflect the hope and peace of Christ that I hold within my own heart.

God's Heart for Justice

As a Christian immigration lawyer, I also seek to live out Micah 6:8: "He has told you, O man, what is good; and what does the Lord require of you but to do justice, and to love kindness, and to walk humbly with your God?" God's great love fills me with his compassion for the oppressed, the poor, and the downtrodden as I listen to each of my client's stories with two sets of ears. First, I draw on my professional capacity to write down information and record any evidence that will help them "win" their legal cases. The other set of ears, which I hope will always remain sensitive, listens to their stories with the heart of Christ. I pray that both my quiet listening and precise words of legal advice will be not only useful to my client's situation, but will also build them up with encouragement, hope, and a peace that surpasses all understanding. As clients often tell me, "*I feel much better after talking with you.*" In this way, I hope to reflect God's heart of justice, kindness, and humility in every conversation.

Jesus for the Immigrant

In Scripture, God reveals his love for immigrants and calls his people to love them as well. So "when a stranger resides with you in your land, you shall not wrong him. The stranger who resides with you shall be to you as one of your citizens; you shall love him as yourself, for you were strangers in the land of Egypt" (Leviticus 19:33-34). This principle, first given to Old Testament Israel, can be applied in some measure by new covenant believers today. Whether we agree with the way immigrants have arrived in our country, they now reside with us in the land. Therefore, we are not to do them harm, but should love them and treat them kindly as we do our fellow citizens. They are now among our neighbors whom God's Word tells us we should love just like we love ourselves (Matthew 22:39).

As I cultivate my heart to care for immigrants, I look for practical ways to express this in my daily life. Most of my clients are educated professionals or well-off investors. They do not have financial needs or much in the way of life's challenges, but nearly all of them are spiritually lost. Like many people in the world around us, they lack a personal relationship with Jesus. So I seek to show them Christ's love in word and deed (1 John 3:18). A different group of clients, however, comes into my office without sufficient funds or business connections. They have little hope for the future and often try to hide their shameful pasts. Many in those precarious situations no longer possess the legal right to remain in this country or else they face the possibility of losing that right. Immigrants who make it to the U.S. without proper documentation also face a life in the shadows with barely any better hope or opportunities than back home. Yet they continue to come, and many are now here.

So, whatever our political opinion, how do we minister to the undocumented people who live in our community, join our churches, and even become close friends? We discover the answer in Jesus' authoritative command: "Go therefore and make disciples of all nations, baptizing them in the name of the Father and of the Son and of the Holy Spirit, teaching them to observe all that I have commanded you" (Matthew 28:19-20a). We must make disciples of Jesus not only by going into all the world, but also by ministering in our cities where the world has come to us. What will we do to further Christ's Great Commission in our own communities and churches where so many from all the nations have gathered? Let us not be reluctant or afraid to do what Christ has commanded, for he has promised to always be with us to the end of the age (v. 20b).

The church begins by removing labels, politics, and poll rankings which can cloud the immigration issue. Instead, we ought to focus on evangelizing people in our community regardless of their status, for Jesus receives all people as his own when they place their trust in him (Galatians 3:28). The church must also be sensitive to those who fear their inability to remain in this country. We teach them that God has a future and a hope for them. We minister to the poor through benevolence and the "one another" care of food pantries, temporary housing, and biblical counseling. We bind up the brokenhearted by showing them a Savior who invites them to cast their burdens upon him (Matthew 11:28-30). The church welcomes the unwelcomed; loves the unloved; cares for the uncared for; and shines like lights in the darkness as we point all people to the person of Jesus Christ (5:14-16).[1] The church's mission to "be Jesus" to the immigrant will bring the immigrant to Jesus, for neither the world nor this nation is the believer's final home. This earthly realm is only entrusted to us for a time which will one day end with Christ's return. Then, at his name, "every knee should bow, in heaven and on earth and under the earth, and every tongue confess that Jesus Christ is Lord, to the glory of God the Father" (Philippians 2:10-11). On that final day, regardless of our nationality or earthly citizenship, all those who believe in Jesus will be welcomed to our new and glorious home.

When I stop and think about all the blessings God has bestowed on me these fifty-five years of life so far, I count being an immigration lawyer as one of the greatest. I rejoice how the Lord has blessed me so that I may in turn be a blessing to others.

Questions for Reflection:

1. How would your life be altered if you grew up in a foreign country in which your culture, ethnicity, and language were the minority?

2. What is the church's responsibility to care for immigrants today? What if they are undocumented? How must the church think differently on these issues than the world?

---

[1] Learn more about a Christian approach to immigration from Matthew Soerens and Jenny Yang, *Welcoming the Stranger: Justice, Compassion, & Truth in the Immigration Debate* (Downers Grove, IL: InterVarsity, 2018).

DEEP FAITH IN THE DEEP SOUTH
Melanie Martin

The elderly couple glared in disgust from the other side of the restaurant as they ordered comfort food from an identical menu as us. I couldn't overhear their comments, but I could feel their hatred burning down the back of my neck. As a bi-racial couple, my husband, Joseph, and I had received plenty of stares in the past, but it bothered me whenever it still happened. Joseph was more used to it, being of mixed race himself, black-and-white, though he always connected more with his black heritage. He has also taught me to remain constantly aware of race as we raise our four boys amidst the jarring reality of daily life in the Deep South.

Becoming the Minority

In May 2020, our family left behind everything we knew on the West Coast and ventured out to the middle of Mississippi to plant a church. Living in Jackson, with its prominent black culture, has been the first time I've ever felt like a minority. After each worship service, our church members often hang about for food and fellowship. Yet along with sharing ethnic cuisine, many of our friends share stories about "life in the hood" and tales of their rough upbringing. They colorfully describe what it was like to grow up in poverty and to rise above the broken homes in their all-black neighborhoods. Even lighter topics like how to braid black hair or where to get the latest "weave" are still foreign to me. So my newfound friends have graciously educated me about all things uncommon as I learn to understand a whole new culture. They help me look beyond the differences of our skin tones and personal preferences in order to behold a far greater beauty in the church.

Invisible White Culture

I grew up in what seemed like the absence of culture. Our military family moved every few years to a different place where I met countless children from all sorts of ethnic backgrounds. Yet despite my exposure to these differences, I wasn't particularly sensitive to the connection most people had with their culture. I'd always felt that "white culture" didn't really exist because we never talked about it or celebrated it. We had a common shade of skin, but we were not bound together by common cultural ties like other ethnic groups. In Midwestern America, our white European heritage simply blended into one since we all looked more or less the same on the outside.

Life's Many Colors

Our family attended Lutheran churches as we moved throughout the Western and Midwestern United States. Each of these churches from California to Montana to South Dakota were led by non-minorities and most, if not all, of the members were white. Despite the lack of diversity, however, it was a blessing to grow up in a believing community. I loved meeting with God's people, singing hymns, and memorizing Bible verses. None of the churches my family attended were perfect, but they introduced me to spiritual disciplines that now, as a genuine believer, I hold dear to my heart. I learned about who God was and how Jesus had died on the cross. Yet sadly, all of that information remained head knowledge instead of becoming truths I cherished in my heart. It wasn't until my early 20's that God truly gave me the desire to know and love him. I had been trusting in my own good works rather than in Christ's, so I thought I was a pretty good person. But then, I realized, according to the Bible, that no one can be good by human effort and no one truly seeks for God (Romans 3:10-12). At the age of 23, I repented of my self-righteousness and turned to God in true faith for the first time in my life.

As a young Christian, I began attending a church in Arizona which built a firm foundation for my faith. During that season, I also served in a crisis pregnancy center where I was blessed to share my newfound faith with ladies from different walks of life, different ages (between 13 and 54), and many different cultures. Some of these ladies who came through our door to receive assistance were refugees from countries like Nepal and Somalia. They couldn't speak much English and they were too poor to even purchase baby food. So free services such as pregnancy tests, parenting classes, counseling, diapers, and clothes, allowed us to tangibly share the love of Jesus and to help these ladies choose life for their unborn babies. I will never forget the young mother who was so adamant that she could not have another child and claimed that abortion was her only option. I shared information with her about the services we offered and prayed with her before she left, but I felt crushed by the choice she was planning to make. Less than a year later, however, she stepped back into our clinic holding her beautiful baby girl. Then she shared with us how our conversation that previous day had helped her see the precious baby in her womb as a gift from God. She had decided to continue with the pregnancy and now could not imagine life without her daughter. Those two years of serving in the New Life Pregnancy Center formed in me a love for helping women regardless of their background, social class, or skin color.[1]

Joseph and I were still new believers when we made the transition to another church that continued to grow our faith. Christ's Church of Tucson (CCT) was my first real taste of expository preaching which centered on and revolved around God's Word. In addition to receiving consistent biblical instruction, I also met with older women who showed me how to be a godly wife and mother. Joseph and I are grateful for our time at CCT, but we also realize that it was still primarily a white church. Just as with my childhood experiences, our season at CCT did not push me to think about race as it related to the church. We only grew close to a few minorities like Raquel, one of my best friends to this day, who had spent most of her life growing up in Hermosillo, Mexico. Raquel shared openly about her culture and we celebrated together the day she passed her test for citizenship. My kids grew up calling her *"Tia"* (Auntie) and treating her

---

[1] Today, about 13% of the U.S. population is African American, but over 30% of aborted babies are black. Some claim this disproportionate access to "reproductive rights" as evidence of socioeconomic disparity, while others view it as ethnocentric oppression, however well-meaning. See Jasmine L. Holmes, *Mother to Son: Letters to a Black Boy on Identity and Hope* (Downers Grove, IL: InterVarsity Press, 2020) for a balanced Christian perspective.

like family. Raquel also taught me Spanish phrases, cooked delicious Mexican food, and always brought a smile to my face. She still passionately loves Jesus and keeps encouraging me to do the same. Her friendship has shown me firsthand how God could create two people so uniquely different, but still knit our hearts together in the Lord.

Vanilla and Cinnamon

During those six years at CCT, God also grew my husband's heart for pastoral ministry. So, in 2016, Joseph accepted God's direction and our family moved to Los Angeles to attend The Master's Seminary. Our stretch in California proved to be an intense time of learning and growth for Joseph, but God had some training in store for me as well. Prior to seminary, we often heard about the kind of "education" which God provided beyond the classroom, but we never could have anticipated the difficulties we were about to face. Our first couple of years were filled with many trials as we suffered from health-related issues, financial pressures, and time constraints. Joseph was physically away from the home far more than I ever thought as he worked night security for Grace Community Church and attended seminary during the day. Thankfully, I was not left alone during that difficult season once I joined the Seminary Wive's Fellowship. A few of us were in the same boat with husbands who worked at the church and spent long hours in study. So we quickly came alongside to encourage each other as we all cared for young children and supported the calling of our husbands.

Sem Wives became my first major exposure to different cultures as I met ladies from many other countries. One of those women, also named Melanie, soon became a close friend. As a Puerto Rican from Philly, Melanie was a ball of energy with a dash of spicy attitude. We even nicknamed ourselves Vanilla and Cinnamon (and I bet you can't guess who's who). Melanie's passions are often on full display and impossible to ignore. Yet her love for the Lord, her husband, and her kids are continuously evident. The two of us also befriended Tarryn from South Africa. So, on Friday evenings, as our three husbands worked the night shift, we forged a lasting friendship. We laughed and cried as we experienced life and learned about each other's cultures over tasty rooibos tea, a South African staple. These good friends also helped me realize how the gospel has no boundaries. Although our skin color and accents were uniquely different, Christ brought us closer than family. Our shared relationships in Jesus Christ bridged any differences in our backgrounds and cultural dynamic. Those times together carried me through many hardships in seminary and also prompted me view my Christian faith through a more global lens.

Greenhouse Growth

Despite the multiethnic experience at Grace Community, I still did not learn how it felt to be a cultural outsider until my husband became a Greenhouse church planting resident at New Life Church in Woodland Hills. The leadership was predominantly Asian American and presented us with new insight into how the gospel transcended race. From our initial visit, we felt as though we had been there for years. We were instant family even though many of us looked nothing like each other and could not relate to the different cultures. My new friends taught me their traditions and introduced me to their favorite foods from various Asian countries. Most importantly, we shared a common bond in our love for Christ.

New Life would eventually celebrate Joseph's graduation from seminary, then send us out with many hugs and tears to plant our church in Mississippi. We were no longer simply friends, but had become a family through the power of the gospel. This beautiful unity could only take root because of our shared salvation in Jesus Christ.

Planting Roots

Our family now lives in Jackson, Mississippi where we have helped to plant a church with a leadership team as diverse as our congregation. My husband is of mixed race, while one elder is white and the other black. Our congregation, which God has faithfully grown, displays a similar diversity. On Sundays, we welcome both black families and white families and others of mixed race. Adding to this dynamic, we also come from varying socioeconomic backgrounds. Some members grew up in the inner cities of Jackson, New Orleans, or Memphis. Others come from real southern country and a few from the well-off suburbs. Young families, college students, and retirees gather every week to worship and "do life" together. As a result, we have grown more aware than ever of how our differences highlight our wonderful unity in Christ.

In Jackson, I finally feel like a minority. I am clearly an outsider as a white girl living in a predominantly black city with a mixed-race husband. I do not think or speak like a southerner and I often don't understand the racial tensions all around me. The world says I should feel "some sort of way" about this cultural dynamic. Yet the work of Christ cultivates a supernatural unity within our church as we learn from, love on, and grow together with those whom society claims will never be the same.

I am also thankful that my children don't wear "race-colored glasses." Their love for others in the church and our community is not determined by people's skin color. Black, White, Mexican, or Asian—different is all they know on a daily basis. So I thank God for the uniqueness of the brothers and sisters in Christ that he has given to our church. May we welcome others as they are and look, with childlike love, beyond our skin color and outward differences. Here is the miracle where grace meets race.

Questions for Reflection:

1. What is so beautiful about the diversity of Christ's church? What have you learned from your fellow believers as they uniquely reflect our Creator's image?

2. How do shared meals, common life situations, or ministry partnerships help to bring diverse people together? What responsibilities are on the majority culture to invite? On the minority culture to assimilate?

FROM DARKNESS TO GLORY
Katrina Figueroa

In the decade since I immigrated to the United States, I have not faced a single instance of racial discrimination or slurs. I have come to see, however, that prejudice is a problem in my own heart and among my people. My first job in the U.S. was working for an African American lawyer who had discovered the boxer, Manny Pacquiao. My employer often traveled to the Philippines and had grown accustomed to our people's ways. In fact, he eventually married a Filipina and started a family with her. Yet I remember, one time, my boss joking that Filipinos were racist. I couldn't believe his statement at first. Yet as I reflected more, I realized how it might actually be true.

Teasing Out Brown

A typical Filipino, due to our ancestry, is short in height, with dark skin, and a small, flat nose. Those who descend from the indigenous Aetas (*negritos*), Indonesians, or Malays will also have black hair that might be either kinky or straight. Yet our society's standard of beauty has become largely influenced by our colonizers, particularly the Spaniards. One can see the effects of this in Filipino show business which prefers actors and actresses who are tall and light-skinned with long, straight noses. These half-Filipinos are so often handed leading roles that many full-blooded celebrities have since undergone nose-elongation surgeries and skin-lightening treatments to achieve that desired standard of beauty. Most of the soaps and facial creams in our grocery stores also contain whitening ingredients.

Brown skin, however, remains common among Filipinos. My friends often teased me as a "*morena*" because I tanned so easily and jokingly called my brother, "*choco*" or "*negro*" because he would turn an even darker shade of brown than me. Filipinos are a happy people who make light of almost anything, so we just brush off these comments with a laugh.

Yet a black foreigner, especially a woman, might be offended to be called a "*negra*." We don't always realize how careless words can unintentionally harm (Proverbs 26:18-19).

Opening Our Eyes

I remember having lived in America for only a few weeks when I first saw a black person. I was oblivious to racial sensitivity and jokingly told my aunt, "*Ang negra naman nya!* Her skin is so dark!" My aunt immediately warned me to never use that offensive word "*negra*" in this country and that it was more polite to simply say "black." So since then, I've become more careful when describing people by their appearance.

I have met many friends from different ethnicities since immigrating to this country and have found California to be quite beautiful for its diversity. Yet since I had never experienced racial discrimination myself, I didn't think much about it until the recent media coverage of George Floyd's death and the Black Lives Matter protests. Some of the news may have been amplified and exploited, but many people were clearly passionate about this issue. I began to realize how the problem of race has historically shaped the lives of people in America.

Gangbanging for Jesus

My husband, Gilbert, for example, encountered frequent racism while growing up Mexican in the San Fernando Valley. He was treated fine by his friends and family, but not always by those with societal power. One high school counselor told him to drop out of school because he was just a trouble-making Mexican who would wind up in jail anyway. Another time, a cop hassled Gilbert and his friend simply for sitting outside a park. The officer threatened to put a bullet into each of them, then falsify his report to say that they had been reaching for his gun. Gilbert got pulled over a lot because of his shaved head and skin color since the cops all thought he was a gangbanger. As a result, he struggled to trust people whom he assumed already thought the worst of him. These self-defeating thoughts hindered him from being kind to strangers because it seemed pointless to try to change their minds.

One day, however, God miraculously saved my husband and radically transformed his heart. His church, made up of people from all different races and backgrounds, freely embraced him. They even pushed aside his handshake, so they could give him hugs instead. It was unusual for Gilbert to find immediate acceptance among people who barely knew him, but he made deep friendships in that church and gained some loving mentors. Unlike many friends he knew who had encountered racism in their churches, Gilbert was fully accepted with all of his tattoos, lip piercings, and fears of not belonging. He had never experienced this kind of love before and built amazing relationships with men and women from all around the world. Since the day when God saved my husband and he walked into the church, God's people have welcomed him with open arms.

Joining as One

As I began to explore this topic for myself, Pastor Voddie Baucham's sermons proved helpful. Through his teaching, I learned that we are all one race, but different in ethnicity. We all possess melanin, just in differing amounts. We were all created in the image of God who makes all lives matter, such that every one of us is valuable. Therefore, this issue about race is more than skin-deep, but penetrates all the way to the level of the heart. Discovering these truths in Scripture have helped me to honor other people as equal in the eyes of God and as sinners in need of his grace.

Sometimes I look at people with different colored skin, or hair, or eyes, and smile in wonder at the creativity of our God. I listen to their vocal tones and accents as I stand in awe of him who spoke them into being. I observe their unique cultural backgrounds and admire their strengths and giftedness. Then, the glorious thought of every nation, tribe, and tongue worshiping before Christ's throne fills me with anticipation of his soon return. "Amen. Come, Lord Jesus!" (Revelation 22:20).

Questions for Reflection:

1. How do we naturally form perceptions based on a person's appearance? Look at some of the people in your church and consider what you might assume of them if you met them as a stranger on the street.

2. How can you guard your church against showing partiality, so that you welcome everyone with the love of Christ? What can you do to remove some of those barriers when people attend your church?

A BEAUTIFUL MOSAIC
Kalle Limit

I was born in Canada to a multiethnic family of European stock. Every Easter, we ate perogies for dinner and decorated our home with pussy willows instead of palm leaves. At Christmas, we feasted on sauerkraut and blood sausages, while opening every one of our presents on Christmas Eve. Yet these holiday celebrations were merely traditions carried over from Estonia and Ukraine. Our family did hold onto certain moral values, but I was not raised according to the Bible or with truly Christian standards.

The Seed of Hatred

My parents separated when I was only seven, so I moved with my mother to another city far away. I grew up fairly destroyed because of that event and directed the hatred boiling over in my heart against others. This first led to a poor relationship with my father whose addiction to alcohol was the reason my mother left him. My dad then snorted away our family inheritance on cocaine while I was still a teenager. The more hatred I directed at my dad, however, the more rage I felt toward others until it became like a cancer that spreads throughout the body.

I especially despised people of non-European nationalities. As a young man with a head full of evolutionary theories about humanity, I considered other races as lesser than my own. If evolution were true, then it would seem logical to believe that every race represented different stages of advancement as shown by our physical and cultural uniqueness. Like many before me, I considered Europeans to be more superior and looked down on those of African origin who displayed more melanin than myself. I even formed a connection with a white supremacist in the U.K. who was willing to send me paraphernalia and encouraged me to make vows of violence against other races.

Rags to Riches

I still thought of myself as somewhat Christian because of my values and ostensible morality. I had been baptized and confirmed in the Lutheran church and I attended services from time to time. I thought that being a good person was all it took to be right with God. Yet I did not possess sufficient faith to make a difference in my relationships with the Lord and other people.

For college, I returned to my roots by moving to Estonia where Jesus then changed my life. My brother and I attended a small Christian church which challenged us to read the Bible. At first, it seemed more like a dare, but, as I read, Jesus opened my eyes to the good news of salvation. I learned that I was indeed a great sinner despite all of my perceived morality, since my sin was first and foremost against a holy God. As Isaiah described, all the thoughts of my heart and even my righteous deeds were yet filthy rags (Isaiah 64:6). I realized then that I was on my way to hell where every sinner deserved to go, but that Jesus Christ my Savior had died upon a cross for me (Romans 6:23). Then, after three days in the tomb, Jesus rose to life again to conquer death and to keep his word. I rejoiced that all my sins were covered by his sacrifice and that I was released from all my hate and former bondage.

The gospel melted my heart, made me a new creation, and cleansed every wrong I had ever done (2 Corinthians 5:17). I even sought to reconcile with my father over the phone though we lived in separate countries. I asked him to forgive me for the way I'd treated him and also expressed that I forgave him for the ways he had hurt our family. How could I hold his sins against him when all of mine were washed away? The Lord amazingly restored our relationship and I would visit him almost every year until his death.

United We Stand

My new life in Christ also led to another wonderful happening. I joined an African church in Estonia and grew to love every one of my brothers and sisters in Christ as family, regardless of nationality or skin color. All my relationships changed because of Jesus and my best friends soon became people who looked very different from me. I spent most of my free time with these newfound brothers and realized the truth that all nations had come from just one man—Adam (Acts 17:26). This oneness of origin meant that we were all distant relatives created in the image of God (Genesis 1:26-27), but also inheritors of original sin (Romans 5:12). We all possessed immense value as members of the human race, but also equally deserved God's condemnation. The Lord used this realization to remove the hatred from my heart and to replace it with his love.

In time, I joined an English-speaking church which ministered to international students from all over the world. This too was a glorious picture of the one body of Jesus Christ welcoming all nations, tongues, and tribes (Revelation 7:9). We grew into a loving church family with hearts focused on Jesus and his work in our lives. Yet instead of losing our distinctiveness, we all made valuable contributions to the manifold glory of Christ.

Divided We Fall

My experience of unity in the church reflects a beautiful mosaic which could never be replicated by any human society. In Canada, I grew up surrounded by all sorts of cultures and nationalities. We held up the ideal of diverse people coming together, while still keeping our cultural traditions. Yet as my own failure showed, we often fell short of our own humanistic standards. When I came to the United States, this country's ideal often resembled a melting pot in which various cultures melted into one shared American identity. Yet in the U.S., current events have shown us how this country is divided along race and ethnicity. Protests, crimes, and other issues draw the lines in view of skin color. Even the matter of abortion has turned into one of race. Instead of remaining focused on the lives of unborn babies, some decry a racist agenda to steal reproductive rights from those of certain skin colors.

Even now, when I fill out forms which ask me to declare my race (i.e., Black, White, Hispanic, etc.), I state "Other" and fill in the blank that I am Adamic—from the one man, Adam. Sadly, it seems that many are more keen to divide people based on race than to unite them in the true man,

Jesus Christ. Yet only in the kingdom of Christ will all people unite under one banner, one name, and one Lord and Savior. Jesus alone has called his church to remain one family under one God, our glorious Father in heaven.

Returning Home

My wife, Susanna, and I will soon return to Estonia to plant a church in the Estonian tongue. Many in our home country, as in the United States, are hurting and broken. They have been destroyed by the cruelty of others and are also enslaved by their own personal sin. So, although most Estonians are of European heritage, they can be just as terrible and hate-filled against those who look like them. Their hatred and their acts of violence take many forms.

Healthy churches in Estonia are hard to find and not every church preaches the words of life. I myself would still be trapped in bondage to my hatred if followers of Jesus had not told me about God's love and encouraged me to read the Bible. For this reason, we hope to plant a church which proclaims the only One who can change the hearts of sinners. Only Jesus can cause hateful people (whether Canadian, American, or Estonian) to find true peace, forgiveness, and unity. Thus, we proclaim Christ alone, so that many will find their new life in him and grow into maturity (Colossians 1:28). We all need Jesus, for only in Jesus do we discover our genuine restoration as we prepare for our return to heaven.

Questions for Reflection:

1. Can a person with a consistently racist attitude still be a Christian? Can someone who denies Jesus as Lord still help society move toward reconciliation and justice? Explain your views.

2. If you helped to plant a church in your present community, what would it look like culturally and socioeconomically? Is that what your church currently looks like? Why or why not?

THE GOSPEL STORY

I remember seething with anger as an American evangelist preached against "The Curse of Ham" to Africans I'd come to know as brothers. I've heard respected Christians declare aloud, "*I'd never let my child marry someone of that race*" and I've wept over historical accounts of atrocities committed in the name of Christ. I am no longer shocked by the depth of prejudice in our world, but still it saddens me that sinful pride is so ingrained in us that we are often blind to it (Jeremiah 17:9). It saddens me that many in our churches cannot even talk about these issues and that some care more about our tribal narratives than about the gospel story that knits us all together.

Perhaps you've never thought much in the past about grace and race. As the dominant culture, you've failed to notice as minorities were overlooked or undermined. You never consciously declared, "*I am more valuable than you. I have more worth. I am superior because of race.*" Yet that might be the way you lived or acted before others. Or perhaps, as ethnic minorities, you justified your prejudice against those who'd worn you down. You refused to think the best of brothers and sisters in Christ unless they viewed society just like you. You withheld grace from those who had been graceless and now consider the current climate as a chance to make things even. Like all of us, you tend to favor those who look and speak and act like you.

God's Story

The church must keep on telling God's greater story of redemption because God's story changes everything no matter who we are. It changes the way we see God's people and how we function in society. It changes even how we hope for change and the shape of our solutions. The radical transformation of the early church took place through the lifechanging good news of Jesus Christ long before affirmative action, diversity training, or civic policies. Therefore, we seek positive change in today's society to be the *result* of converted hearts and not the *cause* of them. Striving for peace and justice must not be viewed as works to earn salvation, but rather works to show our faith (James 2:14-26).

God's greater story of good news still transforms the church today into one family, one new man, and one body whose head is Jesus Christ (Ephesians 4:1-6). As John Perkins has written, "There is no institution on earth more equipped and capable of bringing transformation to the cause of reconciliation than the Church. But we have some hard work to do."[1] It is not that our Christian faith is insufficient to address the problems of racial conflict, but that we do not sufficiently walk in step with the gospel truths we know.

One Church (Acts 10-11; Galatians 2)

Acts 10 unveils how the Lord transformed his disciple Peter into a cross-cultural evangelist. Peter had already witnessed the risen Christ and fully believed in him (1:1-3). He had been empowered by the Holy Spirit to preach a gospel sermon which converted three thousand souls on a single day (2:1-41). He had also witnessed the Samaritan Pentecost when the Holy Spirit came down again to welcome half-breed Jews (8:14-17).

To every people

But then, "at Caesarea there was a man named Cornelius, a centurion of what was known as the Italian Cohort" (10:1). Cornelius was an unclean Gentile—a non-Jew—a filthy Roman. He belonged among the overlords who had conquered God's chosen people and flaunted their pagan idols everywhere. Yet God instructed Cornelius the Roman to send for Simon Peter the Jew (vv. 2-7), who, at that time, was praying by himself in the seaside village of Joppa:

---

[1] John M. Perkins, *One Blood: Parting Words to the Church on Race and Love* (Chicago, IL: Moody, 2020), 85.

> And [Peter] became hungry and wanted something to eat, but while they were preparing it, he fell into a trance and saw the heavens opened and something like a great sheet descending, being let down by its four corners upon the earth. In it were all kinds of animals and reptiles and birds of the air. And there came a voice to him: "Rise, Peter; kill and eat" (vv. 10-13).

Peter didn't think twice about a voice from heaven, yet he argued with God about the message: *"I'm a good Jewish boy who has always kept it kosher"* (see vv. 14-16). And let's face it: How many of us would stoop to eat a reptile? Yet God commanded Peter to "kill and eat" and Peter didn't quite know what to think.

Then suddenly, Gentile messengers arrived at Peter's door to inquire about salvation (vv. 17-23), so Peter went with them to meet Cornelius (vv. 24-27). He entered the Roman's unclean home, but did so with pride, "You yourselves know how unlawful it is for a Jew to associate with or to visit anyone of another nation, but God has shown me that I should not call any person common or unclean" (v. 28). We today might not share this same aversion to the Gentiles, but imagine if some white dude walked into a black man's living room: *"You know it's against God's Word for me to be here or even to associate with you, but God told me to stop calling you common or unclean."* That brother's not going to last very long. Yet the Gentiles with Cornelius were so hungry for the gospel that they looked past Peter's bad behavior and listened only to his message (vv. 30-33). Their response convicted Peter "that God shows no partiality, but in every nation anyone who fears him and does what is right is acceptable to him" (vv. 34-35). Thus, Peter and all those who heard his message were transformed by the very same gospel that Jesus lived a perfect life, died a sacrificial death, and was raised in glory after three days in the tomb (vv. 36-43).

> While Peter was still saying these things, the Holy Spirit fell on all who heard the word. And the believers from among the circumcised who had come with Peter were amazed, because the gift of the Holy Spirit was poured out even on the Gentiles. For they were hearing them speaking in tongues and extolling God. Then Peter declared, "Can anyone withhold water for baptizing these people, who have

received the Holy Spirit just as we have?" And he commanded them to be baptized in the name of Jesus Christ. Then they asked him to remain for some days (vv. 44-48).

This mighty work of God became known throughout the church "that the Gentiles also had received the word of God. Yet when Peter went up to Jerusalem, the circumcision party criticized him, saying, 'You went to uncircumcised men and ate with them'" (11:1-3). People were getting saved left and right as God poured out his Holy Spirit, yet some of the Jews could only respond by criticizing Peter for eating with unclean Romans (Peter's own position not too long ago). So Peter rebuked them, *"Look, here's what really happened. God himself converted these Gentiles. If you have yourself a race problem, then take it up with him"* (see vv. 4-17). Peter's bold challenge seemed to make an impact, for "when they heard these things they fell silent. And they glorified God, saying, 'Then to the Gentiles also God has granted repentance that leads to life'" (v. 18). Salvation, whether for Jew or Gentile, required a changed heart that led to changed behavior.

To the ends of the earth

Soon thereafter, Paul and his friends traveled on mission to the ends of the earth (1:8). They were sent out by a church in Antioch, a multicultural congregation (13:1-3), to plant gospel-centered churches throughout the Gentile world (13:4-14:28). But then, certain ethnocentric Judaizers began to cause trouble: "Some men came down from Judea and were teaching the brothers, 'Unless you are circumcised according to the custom of Moses, you cannot be saved'" (15:1). They were still clinging to the old covenant view that Israel alone was God's chosen people and that righteousness came through adherence to the law. So the church's leaders gathered for a council in Jerusalem to discuss whether Gentiles must first become Jews before becoming Christians. Paul rolled in with Barnabas and Titus. Peter presided with James, the brother of Jesus. Then they all decided together that the Gentiles were no longer second-class citizens in God's eternal kingdom (vv. 2-38). Their decision might seem to us like a no-brainer today, but it required a massive shift in thinking for first-century Jews to even admit that Gentiles could be saved (Ephesians 3:1-6).

To those among us

That might have been the end of the matter until Paul encountered another incident at the multicultural church in Antioch:

> But when Cephas [Peter] came to Antioch, I opposed him to his face, because he stood condemned. For before certain men came from James, he was eating with the Gentiles; but when they came he drew back and separated himself, fearing the circumcision party. And the rest of the Jews acted hypocritically along with him, so that even Barnabas was led astray by their hypocrisy. But when I saw that their conduct was not in step with the truth of the gospel, I said to Cephas before them all, 'If you, though a Jew, live like a Gentile and not like a Jew, how can you force the Gentiles to live like Jews?'" (Galatians 2:11-14).

Picture Peter wolfing down pulled-pork sliders, jamming on Gentile music, and even starting to speak their lingo. But then, the Judaizers came to town again and shamed him into rejecting his Gentile friends: "*Stop eating pork and live like us Jews.*" As soon as Paul heard of this, he confronted not the Judaizers, but Peter to his face: "*Brother, you were just eating pork and listening to gospel music. How then can you turn your back on your fellow brothers in Jesus Christ? Don't you remember the council in Jerusalem?*" Perhaps that's not exactly how it all went down, but surely Paul exposed his friend's hypocrisy.

Sadly, we still observe such problems in the church today when we live by law instead of grace. We fear offending others when we don't know how to act or speak, so we don't lean into relationship. We often group together by ethnicity because it's safer. We naturally drift toward those who look and think and act like us. Yet we fail to keep in step with the gospel that God has made us one church family brought together by his grace. So before we focus on race and class and gender, we must celebrate our identity as one united body in Jesus Christ.

One Gospel (Ephesians 2)

Ephesians 2:1-10 displays the glorious picture of the one gospel by which we are saved. Before salvation, Paul described us all as totally depraved:

> And you were dead in the trespasses and sins in which you once walked, following the course of this world, following the prince of the power of the air, the spirit that is now at work in the sons of disobedience—among whom we all once lived in the passions of our flesh, carrying out the desires of the body and the mind, and were by nature children of wrath, like the rest of mankind" (vv. 1-3).

Paul then marveled at God's amazing grace that we did nothing as rebellious sinners, while Christ our Savior accomplished everything. Over 2,000 years ago, he died as a Jew on a Roman cross to pour out grace on you and me and everyone else who puts their faith in him.

> But God, being rich in mercy, because of the great love with which he loved us, even when we were dead in our trespasses, made us alive together with Christ—by grace you have been saved—and raised us up with him and seated us with him in the heavenly places in Christ Jesus, so that in the coming ages he might show the immeasurable riches of his grace in kindness toward us in Christ Jesus. For by grace you have been saved through faith. And this is not your own doing; it is the gift of God, not a result of works, so that no one may boast (vv. 4-9).

All of us are saved by grace and come to Jesus through faith in his mercy and forgiveness. In him, we all are raised to life and promised glory. In him, we serve and do good works: "For we are his workmanship, created in Christ Jesus for good works, which God prepared beforehand, that we should walk in them" (v. 10). Even the good that we have accomplished to this day was rooted in God's predetermined grace. This one gospel then brought the church together as the foundation for Christian unity:

> Therefore remember that at one time you Gentiles in the flesh, called "the uncircumcision" by what is called the circumcision, which is made in the flesh by hands—remember that you were at that time

separated from Christ, alienated from the commonwealth of Israel and strangers to the covenants of promise, having no hope and without God in the world (vv. 11-12).

Instead of flinging insults at each other, Jews and Gentiles embraced their common ground in Jesus Christ. Paul then reminded the Ephesians how, prior to Pentecost, the Jews had been God's covenant people while the Gentiles had been on the outside looking in.

> But now in Christ Jesus you who once were far off have been brought near by the blood of Christ. For he himself is our peace, who has made us both one and has broken down in his flesh the dividing wall of hostility by abolishing the law of commandments expressed in ordinances, that he might create in himself one new man in place of the two, so making peace, and might reconcile us both to God in one body, thereby killing the hostility" (vv. 13-16).

This dividing wall of hostility referred to worship barriers in the temple, for only Jewish men could enter the inner court immediately surrounding the temple. The next court was reserved for Jewish women and only the outermost court for Gentiles. A stone wall then separated the Gentiles from the Jewish courts and bore the inscription, "*Whoever is captured past this point will have himself to blame for his subsequent death*" (e.g., Acts 21). Imagine chiseled on a wall of stone outside your church: "*Asian brother, climb this wall and you have only yourself to blame. Hispanic sister, cross this threshold and your blood is on your hands. First Nation friend, enter at the price of your own foolishness.*" Jewish worship excluded those outside God's covenant and kept them in the "colored section."

Yet Paul declared that the gospel has transformed every one of our Christian relationships. The former dividing wall of hostility has been dissolved by the blood of Christ, so "[you are now] one new man in place of the two." This word for "new" is the Greek word *kainos*—not a newer version, but brand new altogether. Thus, the union of Jews and Gentiles became radically different before Christ's throne on the common ground of grace.

And he [Christ Jesus] came and preached peace to you who were far off and peace to those who were near. For through him we both have access in one Spirit to the Father. So then you are no longer strangers and aliens, but you are fellow citizens with the saints and members of the household of God, built on the foundation of the apostles and prophets, Christ Jesus himself being the cornerstone, in whom the whole structure, being joined together, grows into a holy temple in the Lord. In him you also are being built together into a dwelling place for God by the Spirit (vv. 17-22).

We are therefore one church connected by one gospel through the sacrifice of one Savior, Jesus Christ. We are family members of one household, children of one Father, and corporately filled by one Holy Spirit. This gospel-centered reconciliation retells the fourfold story of the Bible: Creation, Fall, Redemption, New Creation.

Creation

"In the beginning, God created the heavens and the earth. . . . So God created man in his own image, in the image of God he created him; male and female he created them" (Genesis 1:1, 27). As Paul later preached to the Gentiles, we affirm our Creator's sovereign design of one race, not many: "And he made from one man every nation of mankind to live on all the face of the earth" (Acts 17:26). God created only one human race (one *ethnos*) in the garden.[2] He made Adam and Eve as the first man and the first woman in his image to magnify his glory and creative power.

Racism, however, denies that we were made for God—not to elevate ourselves, but to express his glory through our diversity. So our world may claim the primacy of race as power for the oppressors or victimhood for the oppressed. Yet if we ever cease from seeing human beings as persons made

---

[2] Racism (or ethnic partiality) remains a sad reality in our fallen world and rages against our Creator's design of a single *ethnos*. Sociologists will express racism in secular terms, but secular people cannot grasp either the depths of our depravity or the power of God's grace to transform. Both our world's definition of the problem and their proposed solutions have fallen short. So although they can accomplish much good, they cannot achieve the ultimate good. For without faith it is impossible to please God (Hebrews 11:6a).

in the image of God, then we devalue human life and treat our fellow man as just a higher form of animal. No race should be superior by their birth or by their position in the world. Instead, all peoples must humbly rejoice in our Creator's wisdom to save us by his grace. We are "his workmanship, created in Christ Jesus for good works, which God prepared beforehand, that we should walk in them" (Ephesians 2:10). The gospel story begins with creation.

Fall

Man's fall, however, ushered in our spiritual death, trespasses and sin, slavery to Satan, disobedience, fleshly passions, and lustful desires (Genesis 3; Ephesians 2:1-3). Creation united all people as made in God's good image, but the fall would join them also as children of God's wrath. Every person since Adam has been born as a sinner, humbled by depravity, and deserving of eternal death (Romans 6:23a). Yet like fellow prisoners who all face execution, we may still exalt ourselves by putting down others as inferior (James 3:9b). Sin makes us feel uncomfortable with people not like us and separates us from fellow image bearers (Genesis 1:27). Sin cast the first couple from the garden (3:22-24) and divided Cain and Abel (ch. 4). Sin set apart Noah from his neighbors and Ham from his two brothers (chs. 6-8). Sin dispersed the united nations at the tower of Babel and continues to separate diverse tribes today (chs. 10-11). In a fallen world, neither our attempts at unity nor diversity have served to honor God. The biblical definition of racism is worst news than we ever could have imagined: "Everyone who hates his brother is a murderer, and you know that no murderer has eternal life abiding in him" (1 John 3:15).

Redemption

Yet Christ transformed this tragic story by his redemption through the cross. Our Savior died for people from every cultural and ethnic group (1 Timothy 2:3-6). He made us alive together with Christ on the basis of his precious blood and not the color of our skin. He reversed the curse by creating "in himself one new man in place of the two, so making peace"

(Ephesians 2:15). Therefore, as "fellow citizens with the saints" we enjoy our equal standing in God's kingdom. As fellow "members of God's household," we are sons and daughters of the King (John 1:12-13; 11:51-52; 1 John 2:2). As God's new temple, we no longer keep the Gentiles out. Instead, as the church we bring the nations in (1 Peter 2:4-10). Thus, Paul rejoiced, "For I am not ashamed of the gospel, for it is the power of God for salvation to everyone who believes, to the Jew first and also to the Greek" (Romans 1:16).

The story of redemption proclaims God's greater story for the nations (Isaiah 2:2-4; 60:1-18). As our Creator brings us into fellowship with those we think are different, they are actually more like us than we ever could imagine. Grace unites us with all believers by this fourfold gospel truth: created by our God, shattered by the fall, rescued by the cross, and destined to share eternal glory.

New Creation

Our fallen world tries desperately to keep our thoughts from heaven. Yet our Creator will one day complete his story in the new creation: "And they sang a new song, saying, 'Worthy are you to take the scroll and to open its seals, for you were slain, and by your blood you ransomed people for God from every tribe and language and people and nation, and you have made them a kingdom and priests to our God, and they shall reign on the earth'" (Revelation 5:9-10; see 7:9-10). Instead of boring blandness, our God will populate his eternal kingdom with people from the ends of the earth, from unique cultures and generations, speaking every different language. Yet every one of these worshipers will have been ransomed by Christ's shed blood and they will all rejoice before a common Savior. Thus, our unity amidst diversity increases Christ's magnificence as he garners praise from "every tribe and language and people and nation." God's greater story points us unrelentingly to the glories of Christ in heaven (21:22-27).

In view of this, we pray for God to be glorified in his church today—not simply by diversity, but by our gospel-centered unity. We embrace intentionally those brothers and sisters who are not like us by sharing meals and fellowship across our common ground in Jesus Christ. Even if we don't know how to speak or act, we admit our ignorance as we learn. We humbly confess our sins of either overt or covert racism when we have failed to treat others in the church as equals before God. Most importantly, we cross ethnic and cultural barriers to make disciples in our community (Matthew 28:18-20). May the church move toward this glorious reality of every peoples worship around the eternal throne of Christ.

Our Story

How then should we tell our story within God's greater story? How do we "walk in a manner worthy of the calling to which [we] have been called, with all humility and gentleness, with patience, bearing with one another in love, eager to maintain the unity of the Spirit in the bond of peace" (Ephesians 4:1-3)? Consider the following baby steps of grace we can all start practicing today.

Lean in with Love

First, lean into your relationships with love. True change begins with the attitude of our hearts: Are we humble in our speech and gentle with our words? Are we patient when friends have disappointed us? Do we bear with them in love even when it's hard to trust? As we meet those who do not look or think like us, do we move toward them or away? (see Luke 6:32-36). God's story of redeeming grace tells us who we are as image-bearers of our Creator, sinners saved by grace, and one new man in Jesus Christ. So let us lean toward one another with hearts of love. As Jesus commanded his disciples, "Just as I have loved you, you also are to love one another. By this all people will know that you are my disciples, if you have love for one another" (John 13:34-35). Love compels us to discomfort ourselves for the sake of others, to weep with those who weep, to grow in knowledge, and then take action (Matthew 7:12). Love teaches us to be like Christ who left his home in heaven and leaned in toward us when he laid his life down (John 15:13). Love stops to help like the Good Samaritan instead of crossing over to the other side of the road (Luke 10:25-37), for the wounded need more than statistics about Jew-on-Jew crime or an interrogation about why they were traveling on a particular road during a particular time of day. Caring for our neighbor means speaking the truth with love in the appropriate time and place (Proverbs 25:11).

So move toward your fellow Christian and, when they're ready, let them tell their stories. Invite them in your home and share a meal (1 Peter 4:8-10). "Do life" together. Allow your kids to play. Proximity will breed empathy, while distance only breeds suspicion. "Therefore welcome one another as Christ has welcomed you, for the glory of God" (Romans 15:7). Worship and fellowship together, then lean into those relationships with love. Grace begins with the attitude of your heart (Proverbs 4:23).

Listen to Understand

Second, listen first before you speak (James 1:19). Show grace. Make charitable judgments (Matthew 7:1-5). Be patient as you learn each other's language. Listen, as Christ did, to the Samaritan woman, to Saul of Tarsus, to Rahab and to Ruth, to the widow of Zarephath and the Roman centurion. Listening doesn't mean that you affirm, but more so that you care (Proverbs 15:29).

Then learn about the issues not simply to refute them, but to try to understand (Proverbs 18:2, 13, 17). Those conversations might be raw at first and you won't like some things you hear. Yet resist the urge to guard your tribe or correct each other's lived experience. "Love bears all things, believes all things, hopes all things, endures all things" (1 Corinthians 13:7). Love trusts their suffering to be real as we sit awhile in their pain. They must be able to say of us, *"Yes, you have heard me. You have stated my position more clearly than I ever could."*[3]

God's grace also invites these conversations face-to-face—not by email

---

[3] See the suggested resources at the end of this book for further engagement. Although we affirm the authority and sufficiency of Scripture to address racial issues, we still read widely in order to engage with people whom we disagree.

or social media. This way, you can hear their tone of voice and see their pained expressions. You can pray together with an arm around the shoulder or converse while breaking bread. It's hard to hate when you have really looked into a person's face. So listen in order to understand.

Lament with Sorrow

Then third, lament with sorrow as others ache. Lament, like Christ, our great High Priest, who listens to our prayers and advocates on our behalf (Hebrews 4:14-16). When you hear the next report of ethnic violence, grieve. When your sister hurts, lament beside her. When a tragedy strikes because of race, first "weep with those who weep" (Romans 12:15b), for "if one member [of the body] suffers, all suffer together" (1 Corinthians 12:26a). We may not understand all the complexities of the situation and we may not even agree on the extent of the injustice, yet we affirm how we all need help when we are hurting. Mark Vroegop writes, "Lament is a prayer in pain that leads to trust."[4] As we share our sorrows around the cross, they point us to the comfort we can only find in Christ. So, next time, before you quote statistics or play the devil's advocate, remember Christ who wept before the tomb of Lazarus and comforted his grieving friends (John 11). Before he raised the dead and inverted their despair, Jesus lamented with his friends in pain. But even as he did so, he declared the truth, "I am the resurrection and the life" (v. 25a). Jesus grieved, but not as one who had no hope (1 Thessalonians 4:13). He spoke the truth in his lament that he'd return one day in glory as the King of kings and the Conqueror of death (1 Corinthians 15:24-26).

Lament, however, also means that we must grieve when we have sinned against our brothers—when we are contributors to their pain. We might claim, of course, "*I never knew . . .*" when we awake to the injustice

---

[4] Mark Vroegop, *Weep With Me: How Lament Opens a Door for Racial Reconciliation*. Wheaton, IL: Crossway, 2020. Also see Soong Chan-Rah, *Prophetic Lament: A Call for Justice in Troubled Times* (Downers Grove, IL: InterVarsity Press, 2015).

both in history and the present day. Or we might hear our brother say, *"Your words cut me to the heart. You never saw my pain."* Lament confesses particular sins of overt and covert racism, societal abuses of power, and the responsibility we bear for our religious community (e.g., Daniel 9:1-9). Lament will lead us to repent for our ethnic partiality, but promises God's forgiveness for any sorrow we have caused (1 John 1:5-10).

Leverage Your Resources

Fourth, leverage your resources for the good of others. Consider the gifts which God has given you to be the change for others: your time; your wealth; your home; your family; your courage; your wisdom; your church; your prayers. Become the change in at least one way which calls for humble sacrifice. The way you serve should be specific to your gifts:

- Can you tutor children in reading?
- Can you coach some ball?
- Can you foster or adopt?
- Can you improve access to medical care?
- Can you mentor those without a father?
- Can you invest in a micro-business?
- Can you vote?
- Can you fight for justice in the court of law?
- Can you speak for those without a voice?
- Can you care for the hurting?
- Can you choose to live in a racialized neighborhood?[5]
- Can you invite neighbors to your dinner table?
- Can you celebrate "our common union" at the Lord's Table?
- Can you mobilize your local church to partner with another?
- Can you pray?

---

[5] See David P. Leong, *Race and Place: How Urban Geography Shapes the Journey to Reconciliation* (Downers Grove, IL: InterVarsity Press, 2017) for a thoughtful discussion on the way housing and urban development affects quality of life issues and, by implication, gospel access.

If you have any of these God-given resources or giftings, then leverage the talents he has entrusted to you (Matthew 25:14-30). Be like Christ, who moved into the neighborhood for the good of others (Philippians 2:1-11). Be like Christ, who tore down the walls of hostility in our hearts—like Christ, who loved in tangible ways when he healed the sick, and touched the blind, and looked with compassion on those sheep without a shepherd (Matthew 9:35-36). Be like Christ, for "if anyone has the world's goods and sees his brother in need, yet closes his heart against him, how does God's love abide in him?" (1 John 3:17; see James 2:14-18). When you intentionally disadvantage yourself, you will grow in grace. For God's greater story teaches us to leverage our position, our power, and our privilege for the ultimate good of others (Matthew 5:16).[6]

Long for Heaven's Hope

Lastly, long for heaven's hope for this fallen world is not our home (Hebrews 11:13-16). Earthly justice is not the final word and institutions often fail. At times, we will be disappointed even by those we call our brothers. We will lament the daily news and the pressing hardships of our lives. We will grieve at racial tragedies and the waves of violence which often follow. Yet God's redemptive story still declares our longing for the resurrection's hope (1 Peter 1:3-7). Because Christ lives, we have a home prepared for us in heaven (John 14:1-3). Because he lives, we are assured eternal justice and his promised peace. Because he lives, one day racism will be no more—no longer in our hearts or in society.

So, as much as we are able, let's meditate on that slice of heaven in our worship and our fellowship. Let's pray for opportunities to lean in with love, to listen and lament, and to leverage God's gifts for the good of our community (Jeremiah 29:7). Then, even when this earthly life doesn't go

---

[6] Jemar Tisby proposes the ARC of racial justice. Grow in your Awareness of the issues, build new Relationships with diverse people, then Commit to making one change at a time (Jemar Tisby, *The Color of Compromise: The Truth About the American Church's Complicity in Racism* [Grand Rapids, MI: Zondervan, 2019]).

the way we want, let's keep on longing for the hope of our eternal life in heaven. For we will stand one day before the throne of Christ with every nation, tribe, people, and language, declaring in the loudest voice, "Salvation belongs to our God who sits on the throne, and to the Lamb!" (Revelation 7:9-12).

Questions for Reflection:

1. Practice telling your story in relation to the gospel framework of Creation, Fall, Redemption, and New Creation. How might this daily discipline transform your view of grace, race, and the church?

2. Consider the five baby steps of grace described in this chapter. Which category do you struggle the most to do and why? Decide on specific action steps you will take in the coming year.

HELPING PEOPLE CHANGE ON RACE ISSUES

As Christians begin to talk more openly about race, we will find
countless opportunities to counsel one another from the Scriptures. Some
of us might deal with guilt over racial sins we have committed in the past,
while others might stubbornly deny complicity. Some have let unjust
discrimination lead us to wrong thinking, words, and actions. Many more
wrestle with the complex societal issues of our day (i.e., How do we use our
privilege and power redemptively and not abusively? What does justice
and peace look like for those who have been marginalized?) As we seek to
apply the truths of the gospel in our workplaces, neighborhoods, and
relationships, the four-pronged approach of Love, Know, Speak, and Do
provides practical guidance for helping people change.[1]

Love

True biblical counsel begins not with a sermon, but with genuine love
for the person before you (John 13:34-35). Therefore, like Jesus, get
involved in people's lives to seek their good. Clothe your relationships in
humility (1 Peter 4:8; 5:5) as you lay down your time and resources for the
sake of others (John 15:12-13). Perhaps you might move into their
community or join a church outside your comfort zone. You might invite a
neighbor to your home or grab a drink with a coworker. Loving
involvement means learning about other people's culture, traditions, and
language. It means becoming more like them instead of insisting they
become like you (1 Corinthians 9:19-23).

One way to love them well is to listen to their suffering (Proverbs
17:17). Be patient as they tell their story and ask how you can help. Don't
be afraid to name injustice (e.g., John 4), but then walk slowly if the
person has been wounded in the past. Make sure they are able to keep up

---

[1] This process is more fully developed in Paul Tripp, *Instruments in the
Redeemer's Hands: People in Need of Change Helping People in Need of Change*
(Phillipsburg, NJ: P&R Publishing, 2002).

with your good intentions. Hurting people will learn to trust you as they observe your faithful presence. So treat them as your fellow image-bearers before you help them change.

Know

Effective biblical counsel also requires that you know the person in front of you just as well as you know the Scriptures. Therefore, be like Jesus and ask good questions to explore their situation. Do they struggle with sin or suffering? Are they the ones at fault or were they wronged by someone else? What other influences or factors might be at work? What resources do they have to help them change and do they actually desire to be healed (John 5)? "If one gives an answer before he hears, it is his folly and shame" (Proverbs 18:13; see vv. 2, 17). Below are some sample questions to help find out a person's "STOREE." These types of questions will be asked in the regular course of a counseling conversation.

- **S**ituation: Describe your current circumstances. What seems to be the main problem? What kind of help do you seek?
- **T**houghts: How have you typically processed hard situations? What do you wonder about yourself in relation to your struggle? How does it make you feel about others? At those times, what do you do to occupy your mind?
- **O**thers: How are other people involved in your circumstances? In what way does your struggle impact others? What have people done to either compound or alleviate the problem? Describe any healthy relationships in which you are engaged.
- **R**esponse: What have you done so far about this issue? What are your typical actions or responses to this problem (e.g., "I get angry" or "I hide")? When you feel life's pressures, how does it come out?
- **E**motions: Describe your typical daily emotions. What makes you fearful or anxious? What makes you angry or upset? What would make you happy (related to this situation)? What would give you peace?

89

- Expectations: What do you desire (related to this situation)? What would you like to change? What are you getting that you don't want? What do you want that you're not getting? What do you think you need (e.g., love, respect, justice)? What do you hope will happen through counseling?

Once you have listened to a person's STOREE, then process it biblically before offering wise counsel.

- How is your friend relating to the Lord and to other people (Matthew 22:37-39)?
- Are they habitually manifesting the fruit of the Spirit or the deeds of the flesh (Galatians 5:19-23)?
- Is their underlying heart motive to glorify God (Psalm 115:1)?
- What desires govern their thinking, emotions, and behavior (Proverbs 4:23)?

"The purpose in a man's heart is like deep water, but a man of understanding will draw it out" (20:5). So don't assume you have understood them, but instead ask them if you have rightly assessed their struggle. By the end of the conversation, they should be able to say, "*Yes, you have heard me and you have diagnosed my heart correctly.*"

Jeremiah 17 describes two kinds of people. The "shrub in the desert" trusts only in himself and human resources. His heart is turned away from God and his life will bear the curse of sin (v. 5). He produces thorns, then withers, beneath the desert "heat" of troubling circumstances. So how will he respond to the next atrocity captured on social media? What does she say if labelled a racist? How might the family cope if the bank rejects them for yet another loan? The "shrub" reacts sinfully when sinned against, as "the evil person out of his evil treasure produces evil, for out of the abundance of the heart his mouth speaks" (Luke 6:45b).

On the other hand, the blessed person who trusts in the Lord, "is like a tree planted by water, that sends out its roots by the stream, and does not fear when heat comes, for its leaves remain green, and is not anxious in the year of drought, for it does not cease to bear fruit" (Jeremiah 17:7-8). His character is strong. His roots go deep as he drinks the living water of God's Word (Psalm 1:1-3). He is never anxious in the day of trouble, but rather bears good fruit (Galatians 5:22-23) and offers comfort to those around him. She holds her head high though all the other kids have called her names. Her family prays for the neighborhood bullies who smashed their front window with a brick. They show grace even to their persecutors as they speak against injustice. The blessed "tree" responds like Jesus (1 Peter 2:23), for "the good person out of the good treasure of his heart produces good" (Luke 6:45a).

As you rely upon God's Spirit to discern a person's heart (Jeremiah 17:9-10), you must then identify how they can grow in sanctification:

- Do they need to learn particular truths about who Jesus is or what he has done for them (Ephesians 4:21b)?
- What aspects of their life still reflect the old self (v. 22)?
- What gospel principles will help to renew their mind (v. 23)?
- How can they practically put on the new self and grow into the likeness of Christ (v. 24)?

Speak

You must love them well and know them fully. Then compassionate biblical counsel eventually means that, like our Lord, you will speak "the truth in love" (Ephesians 4:15). Begin by presenting encouragement from the Scriptures, for many who struggle with racial strife have grown weary of the fight (Isaiah 40:30). They have lost hope that society can change or that hateful people can be transformed. So exhort them to "wait for the LORD [to] renew their strength; they shall mount up with wings like eagles; they shall run and not be weary; they shall walk and not faint" (v. 31). Inspire them with the hope that God's Word can accomplish lasting change: "For whatever was written in former days was written for our instruction, that through endurance and through the encouragement of the Scriptures we might have hope" (Romans 15:4). Offer hope to those who suffer the afflictions of others (2 Corinthians 4:7-10) and hope to those who have reaped the cost of sinful choices (Galatians 6:7-8). Offer hope that God's "divine power has granted to us all things that pertain to life and godliness, through the knowledge of him who called us to his own glory and excellence" (2 Peter 1:3). Direct such hurting people to the only source of lasting hope in Christ.

Faithful biblical counsel also instructs people to apply God's Word in concrete ways that bring about lasting change (2 Timothy 3:16-17). As you do so, you must treat them according to their nature: "And we urge you, brothers, admonish the idle, encourage the fainthearted, help the weak, be patient with them all" (1 Thessalonians 5:14). Discern if a person is foolish or rebellious, sufferer or sinner, Christian or unbeliever. Assess whether they sin because of racial ignorance, indifference, insensitivity, or idolatry. Then minister God's truth with patient wisdom as you strive to "present everyone mature in Christ" (Colossians 1:28).

If a person struggles with racist thoughts, words, or actions, you can guide them through the Scriptures on prideful partiality (James 2:1-9). Remind them of their fourfold unity in the church with those who have been made by God, shattered by the fall, rescued by the cross, and destined to share eternal glory. Help them to understand the meaning and the shape of biblical texts which condemn racism as a sin for which our Savior died (Romans 5:8; 6:23). Warn them against cursing others made in our Creator's likeness (James 3:9) and against the rash words which wound like "sword thrusts" (Proverbs 12:18). Then show them how to meditate on Scripture and to capture their every thought in obedience to God's Word (2 Corinthians 10:5). Most importantly, direct them to discover the joyful freedom of repentance: a change of heart that leads to changed behavior (7:9-11).

If a person has endured discrimination, you can guide them through the Scriptures in which our sinless Savior suffered as you call them to suffer "in his steps" (1 Peter 2:21-22). Walk them along the countless passages proclaiming our Father's heart for peace and justice—if not in this present life, then surely in the next (e.g., Amos 5:24). Help them to release any bitterness or unforgiveness to the Lord (Matthew 6:14-15), then teach them how to love their enemies, to pray for those who persecute them (5:44), and to be angry at sin without sinning themselves (Ephesians 4:26a). Remind them of their own identity as a new creation and a reconciler in Jesus Christ (2 Corinthians 5:17-18), for only through Christ Jesus can the racist be forgiven (Psalm 103:10-12) and the sinner born again (1 John 3:8-9). You must instruct them in these truths with love, then trust God's Word to radically change their heart (Hebrews 4:12-13).

Do

As a person understands and receives the Scriptures, teach them, like Jesus did, to build their lives on that permanent foundation (Matthew 7:24-27). Then urge them to implement lasting change: "But be doers of the word, and not hearers only, deceiving yourselves" (James 1:22). Instead of simply acknowledging the proper path, they must take some initial steps: "In all toil there is profit, but mere talk tends only to poverty" (Proverbs 14:23). For some, this might mean offering or asking forgiveness. It might involve reaching out to a person of a different culture or socioeconomic background. It might look like inviting a family into their home whom they had previously avoided at church. Such practical actions must be rigorously specific in order for specific changes to occur.

Supply them also with practical projects for growth as they focus on the "how" as well as the "what" of biblical transformation (Hebrews 3:13). Trust that as they apply God's Word, they will continue to grow and change (Proverbs 4:18). Some suggested categories may include selective Scripture reading, meaningful Bible memory, books and resources pertinent to their struggle, actions which direct them to the heart of Christ, church involvement, and courageous prayers for themselves or others. Exhort them to continue practicing these spiritual means of grace as they walk in step with God's Spirit and his Word (Galatians 5:25).

Finally, help them to integrate these biblical practices until change becomes habitual. Encourage them to seek discipleship in a local church which faithfully studies and applies God's Word (Romans 12:4-16), so that they soon become just like the company they keep (Proverbs 13:20). The wholeness of an integrated life means welcoming others in the church and inviting them into their home. It involves putting off prejudicial thoughts and putting on those renewed by Christ. Their words and actions must reflect their Savior's kindness just as their eagerness to forgive reflects his grace. Like Christ, they will then make sacrifices in their humble desire to bring about justice, peace, and reconciliation.

Integrated change is rarely swift. It requires prayerful wisdom and the commitment to get involved one person at a time. Yet as believers, we offer hope in Christ and through his Word to the worst of sinners and the most wounded of sufferers. We ask good questions until we know a person well and understand their heart. We then instruct the truth in love and teach them how to "do the Word" in practical, specific ways. Helping people change on race requires steadfast reliance on God's grace and the power of his Spirit. Yet he promises to accomplish genuine unity amongst those whose hearts are one (John 17:20-21). Therefore, "may the God of hope fill you with all joy and peace in believing, so that by the power of the Holy Spirit you may abound in hope. I myself am satisfied about you, my brothers, that you yourselves are full of goodness, filled with all knowledge and able to instruct one another" (Romans 15:13-14).

Questions for Reflection:

1. How have you become more like Christ despite your previous views on race issues? Who were some of the influential people in your transformation and what did they do to impact you?

2. Identify one person you are helping to change on race issues. Using the framework of Love, Know, Speak, Do, develop a strategy for walking them toward change.

APPENDIX 1: WORKING DEFINITIONS[1]

Ethnicity – "A word that refers to the way people identify with each other based on commonalities such as language, history, ancestry, nationalities, customs, and values. In the Bible, the Greek word *ethnos* in the New Testament can refer to people groups (who, most basically, would recognize 'us' as being different from 'them') but can also refer to a nation. In Matthew 28:19 Jesus referred to 'all nations' (all *ethnē*)."[2]

Gospel – The good news that a loving God sent his Son, Jesus Christ, to live a perfect life on behalf of imperfect people (Romans 5:8, 19), to die a sacrificial death as their sin deserved (6:23), to rise bodily in victory (1:4; 6:3-5), and to reign forever in heaven with the promise of eternal life for all who repent of sin and trust solely in his work for their salvation (10:9, 13).

Justice – "Biblical justice is characterized by: radical generosity (giving one's resources willingly and sacrificially to those in need), universal equality (treating every person with the same respect regardless of class, race, ethnicity, nationality, gender, or any other social category), life-changing advocacy (using one's power, privilege, or position to speak up on behalf of the poor, oppressed, abandoned, or marginalized in society), and asymmetrical responsibility (accepting and confessing both individual and corporate responsibility for the sins against and resultant suffering of our fellow image-bearers)" (Isaiah 30:18; Micah 6:8).[3]

Multiethnic Church – "A congregation of baptized believers who gather regularly in one place for the administration of the Word and the

---

[1] These definitions are meant to be a starting place for conversations. As such, they are drawn mainly from Scripture or from Christian thinkers who have helpfully engaged both sides of the issues. Seek to begin your conversations about race by first defining your definitions.

[2] Isaac Adams, *Talking About Race: Gospel Hope for Hard Conversations* (Grand Rapids, MI: Zondervan, 2022), 183.

[3] Adapted from Timothy Keller, "Justice in the Bible," *Life in the Gospel* (Fall 2020), accessed at https://quarterly.gospelinlife.com/justice-in-the-bible.

sacraments of baptism and the Lord's Supper . . . in which one ethnicity does not make up more than 80 percent of the whole congregation."[4]

Peace – The biblical promise of *shalom*, describing our unity or completeness in relationships with others, tribes, nations, and, ultimately, God in heaven. Perfect peace, though experienced in part today, will ultimately be accomplished in glory when Christians dwell forever in the presence of Jesus Christ, the Prince of Peace (Isaiah 9:6; 26:3).

Race – A word that can refer to "the human race or a specific ethnic group, but which can be falsely used to mean a category of people with an inherently different value than other people" (Acts 7:19; 17:26).[5]

Racism – "The belief that certain ethnic groups possess less intrinsic worth, dignity, and value and can be classed based on the superiority of one ethnic group over another" (e.g., Numbers 12:1; John 4:9).[6]

Sinful Partiality – Wrong thinking or doing against both God and fellow image-bearers when we elevate our status over another person or group on the basis of age, ethnicity, social class, gender, creed, or other such artificial divide (e.g., James 2:1-9).

Systemic (also called Structural or Institutional) Racism – "A system within a society or organization in which the laws or practices are formed often within an overtly racist society with implicit or explicit racial prejudice, bias, or hatred to segregate, discriminate, or debilitate one or more groups based primarily on their ethnic makeup" (e.g., Acts 6:1-7).[7]

---

[4] Adams, *Talking About Race*, 183. This definition is a general standard of sociologists, though not mandated by Scripture.

[5] Curtis A. Woods and Jarvis J. Williams, *The Gospel in Color for Parents: A Theology of Racial Reconciliation for Parents* (Vancouver, WA: Patrol, 2018), 42.

[6] Phillip Holmes, "Individual Racism vs. Systemic Racism" in *As In Heaven*: a podcast interview with Jim Davis and Justin Holcomb (October 29, 2020), accessed at https://www.thegospelcoalition.org/podcasts/as-in-heaven/individual-racism-systemic-racism.

[7] Ibid.

APPENDIX 2: A LETTER TO MY CHILDREN

My beloved children,

In your lifetime, you may hear of Asian Americans being mocked or harmed because of their cultural or ethnic origin. You might also be shocked when you experience it personally. I pray this will not be a common occurrence, yet it still remains a painful scar throughout our nation's history. So I want to share with you certain truths from the Word of God to help you think rightly about these matters.

Know You Are Loved

First, know that you are loved. Your mother and I love you very much (Psalm 127:3-5) and, though it may not always seem like it, your siblings also love you (Psalm 133). You have many friends and a supportive church family (Colossians 3:11). Most importantly, God loves you so much that he gave his Son to die for you (John 3:16; 1 John 4:7-11) and he created you to reflect his image in your own unique and special way (Genesis 1:26-28; Psalm 139:13-16). So remember that you are loved. Even when hateful people say or do things to harm you, it cannot change your identity before God or diminish your value in his eyes (Romans 8:35-39).

Be Wise in Your Response

When people sin against you as eventually they will, be wise in your response (Colossians 4:5-6). Sometimes it is best to ignore the fool (Proverbs 26:4). Shake the dust from your feet instead of casting your pearls before swine (Matthew 7:6; 10:14). At other times, the ignorant might benefit from instruction (Proverbs 26:5), for "he who listens to reproof gains intelligence" (15:32b). When necessary, you might also seek help from the authorities (e.g., your teacher, your boss at work, the police) who have received God's power to establish peace and justice (Romans 13:1-4). In rare occasions, your wisest response will be to fight or protest, especially to defend those who can't protect themselves (Proverbs 31:8-9).

Our God does not permit you to sin against those who sin against you, but his Word will grant you wisdom for every challenging situation (23:19).

Trust Our Sovereign God

As you face adversity, trust that our God is both sovereign and good (Isaiah 46:9-10). Racism was a normative experience for grandma's father. He lived through the Chinese Exclusion Act and had to take a stranger to be his bride. Gong-Gong did not know the Lord at first, but he witnessed Christian love as generous people drove his children to church every Sunday and when the pastor visited him in the hospital after a surgery. Your great grandpa put his faith in Jesus after he experienced the first act of genuine kindness ever shown him by a white man. So although we may not see the reasons behind our suffering, we trust that our God remains both sovereign and good: "And we know that for those who love God all things work together for good, for those who are called according to his purpose" (Romans 8:28). He will make all things right—if not in this life, then ultimately in the life to come (Revelation 21:1-5).

Rehearse the Good News Daily

My children, fallen sinners will often sin against you (Romans 3:10-12), perhaps because of your skin color or because of cultural stereotypes. Yet remember that you and I are also sinners, "for all have sinned and fall short of the glory of God" (v. 23). We must not view other people's sins of partiality as more deserving of God's judgment than our own pride or discrimination against others (Matthew 7:3-5; Romans 6:23). We all need to know the Savior who promises to forgive our sin when we place our trust in him (Romans 10:9, 13). Not only that, but Jesus also heals us from the shame and scars resulting from racial hatred (10:11). He knows personally how much it hurts to endure such unjust suffering (Hebrews 4:15), yet he refused to channel sinful anger against those who first reviled him (1 Peter 2:21-24). So rehearse this good news daily that Jesus Christ has brought you life (John 10:10b).

Pray Away Your Anxiety

Lastly, don't be anxious about human opinions or run from those who hate you (Proverbs 29:25). Instead, trust God alone to be your refuge (3:5-6; Philippians 4:4-6). Pray for his peace to comfort you whenever you feel afraid (Psalm 56:3) and for his wisdom to guide you when you don't know what to do (James 1:2-6). Pray that God will protect your heart (Proverbs 4:23) and grant you the appropriate words to say (Luke 12:11-12). Pray that those who persecute you might turn to God themselves (Matthew 5:43-45). Then pray that any who still suffer will find their lasting hope in God (Lamentations 3:19-26). "And the peace of God, which surpasses all understanding, will guard your hearts and your minds in Christ Jesus" (Philippians 4:7).

Recount Our Family Story

My beloved children, your heritage also tells the story of God's grace, which now stretches multiple generations in our family history. Recount how grandma's parents sent her to a Christian church and how grandpa learned of Jesus on the other side of America. Consider how daddy grew up in a godly home and how mommy's Christian school teachers showed her how to trust in Jesus. Our family's many stories are a testament to God's abundant grace. I pray then that each of you will add your own stories to this account as still more glimpses of God's greater story for grace, race, and his church.

With all my love,
Daddy

Suggested Resources For Further Engagement[1]

Adams, Isaac. *Talking About Race: Gospel Hope for Hard Conversations.* Grand Rapids, MI: Zondervan, 2022. Also see the *United? We Pray* (podcast), accessed at https://uwepray.com.

Baucham, Voddie T., Jr. *Fault Lines: The Social Justice Movement and Evangelicalism's Looming Catastrophe.* Washington, D.C., Salem Books, 2021. See also The Dallas Statement on Social Justice and the Gospel, accessed at https://statementonsocialjustice.com.

Davis, Jim, and Michael Aitcheson. "As In Heaven: A Conversation on Race and Justice." *TGC podcast series* (Fall 2020), accessed at https://www.thegospelcoalition.org/podcasts/as-in-heaven.

DeYoung, Kevin, and Trent Hunter. *Thinking Theologically about Racial Tensions.* Greer, SC: Heritage Bible Church, 2021, accessed at https://heritagegvl.com/new-ebook-thinking-theologically-about-racial-tensions.

Gay, Jerome, Jr. *Talking to Your Children About Race: A Biblical Framework for Honest Conversations.* Greensboro, NC: New Growth Press, 2022.

Gray, Derwin L. *Building a Multiethnic Church: A Gospel Vision of Love, Grace, and Reconciliation in a Divided World.* Nashville, TN: Thomas Nelson, 2021.

Hays, J. Daniel. *From Every People and Nation: A Biblical Theology of Race.* New Studies in Biblical Theology, Vol. 14. Edited by D. A. Carson. Downers Grove, IL: InterVarsity Press, 2003.

Kellemen, Robert W., and Karole A. Edwards. *Beyond the Suffering: Embracing the Legacy of African American Soul Care and Spiritual Direction.* Grand Rapids, MI: Baker Books, 2007.

Keller, Timothy. "Justice and Race" (4-part series). *Life and the Gospel* (2020), accessed at quarterly.gospelinlife.com/the-bible-and-race.

---

[1] The views expressed by these resources will not always agree with each other, with our church, or even with the biblical narrative. They can, however, help us to better engage in racial issues with both critical thinking and Christian grace.

Linne, Shai. "Gospel Conversations about Race/Ethnicity in Your Church Community." *CCEF Conference on Modern Problems* (2021), accessed at https://www.ccef.org/shop/product/gospel-conversations-about-race-ethnicity-in-your-church-community.

Newbell, Trillia J. *God's Very Good Idea Storybook: A True Story of God's Delightfully Different Family.* Epsom, UK: The Good Book Company, 2017.

Perkins, John M. *One Blood: Parting Words to the Church on Race and Love.* Chicago, IL: Moody Publishers, 2018.

Reyes, Michelle A. *Becoming All Things: How Small Changes Lead to Lasting Connections Across Cultures.* Grand Rapids, MI: Zondervan, 2021.

Sanchez, Juan, et al. *A Biblical Answer for Racial Unity.* The Woodlands, TX: Kress Biblical Resources, 2017.

Sugimura, Tom. *The Church Behind Barbed Wire: Stories of Faith during the Japanese American Internment of World War II.* Amazon, 2022.

Tibayan, P. J., et. al. "Race, Gospel, & the Local Church: Stories of Hope." *SOLA Conference* (2021).

Tisby, Jemar. *The Color of Compromise: The Truth About the American Church's Complicity in Racism.* Grand Rapids, MI: Zondervan, 2019.

Vroegop, Mark. *Weep With Me: How Lament Opens a Door for Racial Reconciliation.* Wheaton, IL: Crossway, 2020.

Williams, Jarvis. J. *Redemptive Kingdom Diversity: A Biblical Theology of the People of God.* Grand Rapids, MI: Baker Academic, 2021.

Williams, Thaddeus J. *Confronting Injustice without Compromising Truth: 12 Questions Christians Should Ask About Social Justice.* Grand Rapids, MI: Zondervan, 2020.

Yancey, George A. *Beyond Racial Division: A Unifying Alternative to Colorblindness and Antiracism.* Downers Grove, IL: InterVarsity, 2022.

55064651R00059